THE 15-MINUTE
PHILOSOPHER

IDEAS TO SAVE YOUR LIFE

ARCTURUS

ARCTURUS

This edition published in 2015 by Arcturus Publishing Limited
26/27 Bickels Yard, 151–153 Bermondsey Street,
London SE1 3HA

ISBN: 978-1-78212-642-3
AD003871UK

Printed in China

CONTENTS

What is philosophy for?

Have you ever sat up late into the night over a bottle of wine, or too much black coffee, discussing the great questions of life? You might have less time and stamina for staying up into the small hours now, but you don't need to wait until dark to give your brain a 15-minute philosophical work-out.

Uses of philosophy

Some people think of philosophy as an ivory-tower occupation with no application to the real world. They couldn't be more wrong. Philosophy lies behind every important decision we make and affects all aspects of our lives. Philosophical thought has created our laws

Philosophers traditionally drink too much alcohol and coffee, smoke too much and stress over the meaning of life.

'What I really lack is to be clear in my mind what I am to do ... the thing is to find a truth which is true for me, to find the idea for which I can live and die.'
Søren Kierkegaard, 1835

and our interpretations of religious texts. The way we treat criminals, how we structure our schools, the placing of CCTV cameras, the presence of GM ingredients in our foodstuffs, how much tax we pay, the availability of porn online, and whether you can have an organ transplant are all philosophical issues. Thinking about ethical, political and metaphysical questions is enjoyable and empowering. It is essential if you want to develop informed views on the critical

Diogenes, c.350BC, Athens: long ago, philosophers had to make do without the coffee and cigarettes. Diogenes made do without most things and lived in a giant jar.

questions of modern life.

Philosophy will help you to work out what you think and why, and enable you to become the type of person you believe you should be. That doesn't mean fulfilling an ambition to become a film star or astronaut – it means knowing what is important to you and living your life by your own set of standards and priorities. There can be no more important or satisfying aim, no better work than person-building, and no better place to start than with yourself and your own, personal brain. It's all you need.

Lots of questions – are there any answers?

If we want to know which of two mountains is taller, we can measure them both and compare the results. If we measure accurately, we will have a definitive answer. Philosophy is not like that. If you say there is a god and I say there is not, we can both present our reasons for thinking as we do but there is no way an objective observer can be certain who is right. We have no way of finding a universally 'true' answer to questions such as the morality of abortion, or whether democracy is the fairest form of government.

With no equivalent of the tape-measure-for-measuring-mountains, how can we test our ideas? We can try to work out through reasoned discussion which of two or more conflicting ideas is better in a

DANGER – PHILOSOPHERS AT WORK

The ancient Greek philosopher Socrates wandered around Athens, teaching philosophy. His frequent debates with the aristocratic youth annoyed the city elders who saw him making young people more troublesome and argumentative than they need be. He was eventually put on trial for corrupting the young and offending the gods. Offered the chance of a reprieve if he would give up philosophy, Socrates refused, further antagonized the court and was sentenced to death. He died in 399BC by drinking the poison hemlock, surrounded by his friends. He is considered the originator of Western philosophy.

Persecution is a perennial danger for philosophers. Totalitarian regimes often turn against the intellectuals in their midst. Mao's China, Pol Pot's Cambodia and Stalin's USSR all imprisoned and abused intellectuals because of their dangerous potential to encourage the populace to challenge the authorities – the same accusation as Socrates faced 2,500 years previously. People who don't think are easy to govern and easy to oppress. Philosophers are the intellectual equivalent of arms dealers in the eyes of an unenlightened state.

joint endeavour to discover the truth, or we can each stubbornly try to persuade others of our point of view by restating it. The first approach is philosophy; the second is unproductive intransigence.

To gain anything, you must come to philosophy with an open mind and a desire to learn, to change or deepen your views. You may, in the end, find you still hold the same views but they will have a stronger foundation as they will be rooted in reason and supported by evidence.

Opinion vs truth

Because there are no definitive, external proofs, some people are inclined to

MEASURING MOUNTAINS

Nothing is as simple as it looks, including the question of which is the higher mountain. In science – as in philosophy – it's important to know what the question means before trying to answer it. Is the world's tallest mountain Mount Everest in the Himalayas? Or is it Mauna Kea in Hawaii? It depends how you measure it...

If you measure from sea level, it's Everest. If you measure from the surrounding plain, it's Mauna Kea (though the plain is the seabed). In philosophy, we are as likely to query the question as the answer.

Is there life elsewhere in the universe? We don't know – but there is a true answer to the question, we just don't have the means to find it.

think that philosophical questions are just a matter of opinion. But the lack of 'right' answers doesn't make a question a matter of opinion. Instead, philosophy consists in setting forth propositions and exploring or defending them through logic and reasoned argument, refuting counter-arguments, and trying to edge towards the best possible answers. These answers might well be overthrown by another argument – just as a theory in physics might later be replaced by a better theory. In physics, a preferred theory is one that better fits the observed phenomena and enables us to make predictions which turn out to be accurate. For an idea to be 'good' in philosophy, it must be consistent, without internal contradiction, inclusive, and, in many cases, universally applicable.

Is it ever true?

If we can't conclusively demonstrate the truth of a philosophical statement, does that mean that we can't say there are philosophical truths? This is a question that philosophers have asked, and – as you might expect – they have come up with differing answers.

The question is not limited to philosophy, either: they also ask it of other disciplines, including physics. Are our discoveries in physics really discoveries of an objective truth, or are they just a convenient way of representing our observations of the world? It is possible that there is truth 'out there'. But that is another matter about which we cannot be sure.

'Killing people is wrong'

Like science, philosophy tries to approach the truth. If we take the statement 'killing people is wrong', we can quickly come up with cases in which some people might not think it wrong – when a terminally ill person in pain asks for release, for example. That makes the proposition not universally applicable, so it needs to be

adjusted. We could refine it to 'killing people against their wishes is wrong'. Again, we might come up with objections. What about war? What about judicial execution? Some people will still hold that the very first statement is true, and could provide arguments to support their view, but others might amend the statement again, perhaps to 'killing innocent people against their wishes in peacetime is wrong'. Through this process of scrutiny and iteration, philosophy hopes to come up with rules and beliefs by which we can live, build societies and relate honestly to the natural world. Perhaps, along the way, it might also discover some truths. Who knows?

PART 1:

THOUGHT

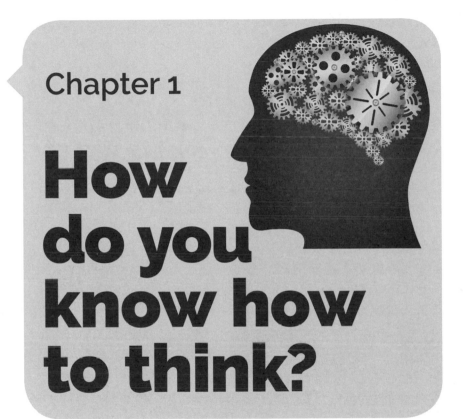

Chapter 1

How do you know how to think?

How, then, do you proceed with philosophical thought?

'Philosophy is a discipline. You've got to discipline your thought. It's not just making stuff up. And disciplining your thought is very hard to achieve.'
Tim Crane, Knightbridge Professor of Philosophy, University of Cambridge

Question everything

Disciplined thinking takes nothing for granted. In the last chapter, we saw that the apparently simple question – which of two mountains is taller? – needs more clearly defining before it can be answered. In philosophy, all questions and all terms must be examined and defined before we can feel secure in proposing answers.

The tools we use to do philosophy are logic and reason; the arguments they produce can only be presented in language. This means that language itself falls under scrutiny. A good part of the philosophical work of the twentieth century went into examining the foundations and reliability of language.

When you begin to look at philosophy, it can feel as if everything is constantly shifting, and questions multiply in front of you. It can be invigorating, or terrifying, or both. If you like certainty, philosophy might not be for you. But if you enjoy mental gymnastics, and don't mind the ground you have built your life on being wrenched from beneath your feet, it might be just what you're looking for.

A fractal is a pattern that becomes ever more complex. The closer you look, the smaller the details you can see as the pattern replicates as it fragments. In mathematics, the area enclosed by a fractal is finite, but has a boundary of infinite length. You can think of philosophy as fractal – every question leads on to further questions.

Dismantling certainty

Socrates often said that the only thing he was sure about was his own ignorance, and that if he was wiser than other men it was in that he recognized his ignorance. Socrates made a habit of challenging people who thought themselves knowledgeable to define common concepts such as 'courage' or 'justice'. He would then present counter-arguments, revealing inconsistencies or contradictions in whatever they said – it didn't matter how they answered, he could always pick holes in what they said. His aim was to show that everything is more complicated than we are inclined to think, and accepting commonly-held beliefs without scrutiny is unwise. That was how he got into such trouble with the authorities in Athens. His way of teaching is known as the Socratic method and is still used. It is a dialectic method – a dialogue framed as a reasoned argument in which logical responses should lead the participants to the truth.

Thesis-building

Although Socrates used dialectic principally to unpick established beliefs, it is also used to build knowledge. Again, it works through a process of questions and answers, the answers prompting new questions that probe further and allow the participants to edge towards deeper understanding.

Dialectic now is often associated with an eighteenth-century German philosopher, Georg Hegel (pictured above). It progresses in three stages:

- **thesis:** this is the idea or statement that is being proposed as true, such as 'lying is wrong'
- **antithesis:** this is a reasoned answer to the thesis, contradicting it, such as 'lying sometimes protects people from harm and so can be good'
- **synthesis:** this is a new statement of the idea, revised in the

light of the objections raised by the antithesis. In the example, it might be 'lying when it is not intended to protect the person lied to is wrong'.

The process can be repeated. The synthesis becomes the new thesis, and is examined and readjusted. By going through these steps, either in dialogue with someone else or by thinking the argument through yourself, you can scrutinize your ideas and make them more robust.

Court cases are tried by debate, with one side arguing in favour of the defendant and the other arguing the case for the prosecution. The skills and methods of philosophical debate are used to determine whether or not someone is guilty of the crime.

Start from scratch

In general, philosophers start with the work of earlier philosophers and use logic and argument to move the debate forwards. But that's not always the case. Philosophy is one of few disciplines in which it's perfectly possible to throw out baby and bath water and run a new bath, starting from first principles. As long as the new model is logical and internally consistent it stands a fighting chance of being taken seriously. Martin Heidegger (1889–1976) and Ludwig Wittgenstein (1889–1951) both

> ## PLAYING DEVIL'S ADVOCATE
>
> In philosophical debate, one person or group might play 'devil's advocate', arguing for a view they don't necessarily support just for the purpose of having a debate. From 1587 to 1983 'devil's advocate' was an official role. In examining the case for making new saints, the claim for the proto-saint was presented by 'God's advocate' and challenged by the 'devil's advocate'. It was the job of the devil's advocate to pick holes in God's case. Socrates played devil's advocate to uncover inconsistencies in the arguments of his opponents.

decided that for two thousand years philosophers had got it all wrong and it was time to start again. Wittgenstein even stated: 'It is a matter of indifference to me whether the thoughts that I have had have been anticipated by someone else.' It certainly saves a lot of time that would otherwise be spent reading up on previous ideas, and can also bring a freshness that allows completely new angles to emerge.

The role of logic

Logic is a very highly formalized way of thinking and reasoning that involves using language as a precision tool. The first philosopher to set out the methods of logic was Aristotle, who lived in Athens in 384–322BC. He showed how we can start with two true statements that share one 'term', and draw another true statement from them, using the terms they don't share. The most famous example of this method – called logical syllogism – is:

> ***All men are mortal. Socrates is a man.*** *Therefore* ***Socrates is mortal.***

Here, the shared term is 'man' – it's in both the first two statements. This can be reduced to something more formulaic:

All As are B. C is an A. *Therefore* ***C is B.***

The third statement remains true even when we remove the content (the details of men and mortality). This shows that the logic is valid: it is a formal relationship between statements. As long as the first two statements are true, the sequence will always work. Logic of this kind cannot be refuted – the difficulty for philosophy is filling in the terms – finding the statements – that lead to useful and meaningful conclusions. This is where we need to be very precise and careful.

Suppose we were to say:

Killing people is wrong. Abortion involves killing people.
Therefore ***abortion is wrong.***

This is open to several challenges. The first is whether 'killing people is wrong' is actually a true statement – there might be circumstances in which killing people is not wrong. The second is whether abortion involves killing people: we have to ask when or whether a foetus counts as a person, and whether we can 'kill' something that is not independently alive. Although the logic is sound, the content is not. To practise philosophy, you need to keep a tight rein on both – to 'discipline your thought'.

Where to start?

The French philosopher René Descartes (who, incidentally, also invented the Cartesian coordinate system used to draw graphs) famously said: 'I think, therefore I am.' It was his starting point for philosophy. He realized that he needed to start from something he could feel sure of, a secure proposition.

The position of certainty he came up with was his own existence, proved by his being able to think. Using Aristotle's system of syllogisms, he could say:

Only things that exist can think. I can think.

Therefore **I exist.**

For most people, the more important and pressing questions in philosophy are ethical questions – these are concerned with what is morally right and wrong. This is the area where we are most likely to encounter philosophical quandaries in our daily lives, and where they will impact on actions. Questions such as whether we should move an elderly relative into residential care against her wishes, or how we should treat animals, probably seem more relevant than if/why anything exists.

Often, this is where you will start – asking what you should do or trying to decide your opinion on a topical issue. But philosophical questions are especially prone to mission creep. Something that starts off as a seemingly straightforward and specific question often has roots that go far deeper – which is why Descartes had to start by establishing that he existed. It is precisely this aspect which makes philosophy so fascinating and rewarding.

Chapter 2

If a tree falls over in a forest, does it exist?

So where can we start? What's real?

> *'What is comprehended by you or I may not be [comprehended] by a cat, for example. If a tree falls in a park and there is no-one to hand, it is silent and invisible and nameless. And if we were to vanish, there would be no tree at all; any meaning would vanish along with us. Other than what the cats make of it all, of course.'*
> William Fossett, *Natural States*, 1754

Is anything real? What do we mean by real? Does anything exist? Can we be sure? And is existing the same as being real?

What's out there?

For a philosopher, nothing is given – we have to prove things, and that includes proving existence.

ABOUT THAT TREE

The usual wording of the tree question is: 'If a tree falls over in a forest and there is no one around, does it make a sound?' The seventeenth-century philosopher John Locke would say that the answer is no. Most scientists would agree: 'sound' is defined by being heard. As the tree falls, it creates vibrations in the air which would be experienced as sound if a hearing observer were present. If you wave your hand in the air, it creates vibrations of the same type as the falling tree, or a ringing bell. The air is moving so slowly that we can't hear hand-waving and so it is silent. It's possible some other creature could hear the sound of a waving hand. The world would be a very noisy place to such a creature.

Descartes came up with his famous saying, 'I think therefore I am', during his attempt to establish what he could be sure of. He felt secure in his own existence because he couldn't be thinking unless he existed. But even that is not really secure. Later philosophers pointed out that all the thinking proved was that thinking was occurring – not that Descartes existed to do it.

Even if you feel secure in your existence, can you be sure anyone else exists? Perhaps you have created the entire external world with all its people and your own past experiences (and this book to prompt you to think about it), and nothing else is real.

DISCOURS
DE LA METHODE
Pour bien conduire ſa raiſon,& chercher
la verité dans les ſciences.
PLUS
LA DIOPTRIQVE.
LES METEORES.
ET
LA GEOMETRIE.
Qui ſont des eſſais de cete METHODE.

A LEYDE
De l'Imprimerie de IAN MAIRE.
cIɔ Iɔ c XXXVII.
Auec Priuilege.

'[Reality] is a controversial concept asserting that "things" are "there" and this is somehow indisputable.'
Uncyclopedia

THE ALLEGORY OF THE CAVE

Imagine a group of people held as prisoners in a cave. They can see shadows on the wall of the cave which are cast by beings and things outside the cave. As far as the people in the cave are concerned, these shadows are reality. The come up with theories to explain how reality works and why things are as they are (= appear to be). If one person were to escape from the cave and see real reality, he or she would at first struggle with it. When they returned to the cave, they would have great difficulty explaining to the other cave-dwellers that what they could see was not reality at all. Plato puts himself in this position, the returned fugitive, as the philosopher trying to explain to humanity that what we see is not top-notch reality, even though it is all we can experience.

Real or idea?

Philosophers who believe reality exists independently of any observers are called realists. Those who think reality is an idea constructed in the human mind are idealists. There are plenty of shades of realism and idealism. The most fundamental realism holds that everything exists and is just as it appears to us. This is the default position for most people – we live our daily lives on the assumption that reality is 'out there' and is how we think it is. Philosophers call this naïve realism. Aristotle was an arch-realist in that he felt secure

that the world 'out there' exists and is real. He also believed that our senses give us a reliable experience of the world. Plato, Aristotle's tutor, had a more complicated view. He believed there were two tiers of 'reality'. One, the superior tier, was the realm of ideal 'forms'. The form is the essence or ideal conception of something – so the perfect horse, the most complete conception of justice and even the best haircut all exist as 'forms'. Unfortunately, the realm of forms is not accessible to us in our imperfect bodies. Instead, we dwell in the second tier of reality, the rather shoddy material world. Here, there are lots of instances (or instantiations) of the forms, but none is very good. The horses aren't super-sleek and super-fast, the justice systems are a bit corrupt, and there are a lot of bad hairstyles. However, it's the only reality accessible to us, so we'll have to make do with it. Plato tried to explain the disparity with what we perceive as reality (the material world) and the purer, high-grade reality of the realm of forms using the allegory of the cave (see panel on page 25 and picture opposite).

> *'The reality of external objects does not admit of strict proof.'*
> Immanuel Kant, 1781

NOTHING EXISTS...

The early Greek philosopher Gorgias (c.483–375BC) took a hard-line, negative view of reality:
- Nothing exists.
- Even if something exists, nothing can be known about it.
- Even if something could be known about it, knowledge about it can't be communicated to others.

This is called a solipsistic view – accepting only the existence of the thinker as certain. (Existing and being real are not necessarily the same thing in philosophy.)

The German philosopher Immanuel Kant (1724–1804) took a slightly similar approach, distinguishing between objects we experience as phenomena – visible, graspable, smellable, apprehendible reality – and objects 'in themselves', which he called noumena and which don't appear in space and time and about which we can know nothing.

Alternative (non)-realities

If you're not convinced reality exists, there are other options to pick, including:

- **'Brain in a vat'** – you are not really a brain in a body walking around. You are a brain kept in a vat of sustaining fluid somewhere. Your brain is fed images and sensations by a computer that has created a virtual reality you now believe is real.
- **'The evil demon'** – an evil demon has you in his control and is persuading you that 'reality' is real.
- **'It's all a dream'** – dreams seem real to us at the time, so how do we know that all our life is not a dream? In the fourth century BC, the Chinese philosopher Zhuangzi woke from dreaming he was a butterfly and asked how he could know which identity was real: was he Zhuangzi dreaming he was a butterfly, or a butterfly dreaming he was Zhuangzi?
- ***The Matrix* is true** – we are inhabiting, or part of, a computer

There is no way of proving that things which seem to be very old were not created recently, endowed with compelling evidence of their antiquity in order to deceive us.

> **'There is no logical impossibility in the hypothesis that the world sprang into being five minutes ago, exactly as it then was, with a population that "remembered" a wholly unreal past. There is no logically necessary connection between events at different times; therefore nothing that is happening now or will happen in the future can disprove the hypothesis that the world began five minutes ago.'**
> Bertrand Russell, 1921

simulation created by some other beings.

- **'It just happened'** – the world was created very recently – perhaps last Thursday. (The theory is sometimes called Last Thursdayism.) Everything in the world, including your memories, has been created to give the impression that it is much older. This is a slightly shorter-term version of Creationism, which maintains that the world was created, with its apparent geological history, only a few thousand years ago.

Putting God in the frame

The Anglo-Irish bishop George Berkeley (1685–1753), who is often falsely credited with asking whether an observed, falling tree makes a

IT'S THERE IF WE BELIEVE IT IS

'Consensus reality' is a term for things or situations that are deemed to be real because most people believe they exist. For example, in some modern and many ancient societies, enough people believe in the existence of a god for the god's existence to count as consensus reality. If people stopped believing in that god, the consensus reality would change. Two thousand years ago, the geocentric model of the universe had the status of consensus reality, but now it's only accepted by a few wackos and ignorant people and is deemed untrue or unreal – reality has moved on.

sound, would have said that not only is there no sound, there is also no tree. But there is no tree in rather a special sense.

For Berkeley, as later for William Fossett, all experience is perceived through our senses – and that is all it is: perception. All that exists is our perception of things and states, internal and external, and things don't exist if not perceived. 'Esse is percipi,' he said – to be is to be perceived. But Berkeley didn't believe that we constructed all these sense perceptions from nothing. As he said, when we open our eyes, we don't choose what to see. The variety of perceptions comes from God. And as God continues to see a tree even when no one else is looking, the

A vehicle travelling over the Moon makes no sound as there is no air to vibrate. Sound needs an interaction of moving thing, air and observer.

> 'I do not argue against the existence of any one thing that we can apprehend, either by sense or reflection. That the things I see with mine eyes and touch with my hands do exist, really exist, I make not the least question. The only thing whose existence we deny, is that which philosophers call matter or corporeal substance. And in doing of this, there is no damage done to the rest of mankind, who, I dare say, will never miss it.'
>
> George Berkeley, *A Treatise Concerning the Principles of Human Knowledge* (1710)

tree continues in the same place for the next person who comes along. It's a neat trick, but demands a lot of God – not least of all his existence.

What are things like?

What we can know of things that exist is always mediated through our bodies – either our senses or our minds (see *What do you know?* Page 38). Again, we are thrown back on perceptions. We describe things as hard or soft, wet or dry, according to our experience of them.

If you were to touch some fur and then touch some steel, you would notice differences between them. The fur is soft and the steel is hard. The fur is warm and the steel is cold. But how far are these real differences, integral to the substances, and how far are they differences only in our perception of them?

Fur and steel, if they have been kept in the same room for a while, are both the same temperature. Fur feels warm because it is a thermal insulator. Steel feels cold because it is a conductor of heat – it draws the heat away from our fingers and so we experience it as cold. Fur feels soft because it comprises lots of tiny, separate fibres that can move in the cushion of air between them. We could make fur from steel, but the way we usually experience steel is as a block, not a steel-and-air mix. Iron filings feel

The elephant 'is' two metres high, but it 'is' noisy and grey only in the presence of a hearing and seeing observer – beauty really is in the eye of the observer.

soft. Of course, there are also genuine physical differences between materials, differences that are produced by the arrangement of atoms and molecules.

John Locke divided the properties of objects into primary and secondary types. The primary properties are those which he felt genuinely belonged to the objects – extension in space, shape, whether they are moving, and so on. The secondary properties are those that depend on our sensory perceptions of the object, such as their colour, how weighty they feel, and the noises they make. The German philosopher Martin Heidegger (1889–1976) believed that our understanding of the world is always in relation to ourselves. He described 'Dasein', literally 'being there', as the state of the human. Our existence is defined in terms of our context in the world and it's impossible to separate our individual consciousness from the surrounding environment.

Quantum thereness

One of the most famous icons (perhaps the only famous icon) of quantum physics is Schrödinger's unfortunate cat. Schrödinger's cat is the

IS THE MOON THERE?

There is a (possibly apocryphal) story that Einstein once asked the quantum physicist Niels Bohr if he genuinely believed that the Moon only exists while someone is looking at it. Bohr is said to have replied that Einstein would not be able to prove that it does.

tree-in-the-forest two hundred years on – possibly one of those cats that was watching the non-tree not falling. In this thought experiment devised in 1935, Erwin Schrödinger suggested that we think of a cat shut in a box (see below). Also in the box is a flask of poison, some radioactive material and a detector measuring radioactivity. If the detector finds evidence of radioactive decay, the flask is automatically broken and the poison will kill the cat. If there is no radioactive decay, the cat will be fine (though presumably angry at being shut in a box with lots of stuff).

The state of the cat (dead or alive) is not known until the box is opened. According to quantum theory, the state of the cat is not even *determined* until the box is open. The cat is *both* dead *and* alive at the same time until its state is fixed by observation. Schrödinger

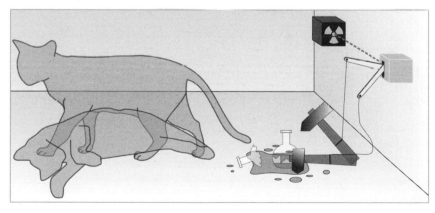

devised the experiment to show how ridiculous some aspects of quantum theory sound when scaled up from the atomic level to the world around us – why is the cat dead *and* alive until its state is *fixed*, rather than dead *or* alive until its state is *known*? It's all to do with the quantum state of entanglement of subatomic particles, but we don't need to look that closely here. The question, as with the tree, is how the presence of an observer impacts on, or indeed creates, what we think of as reality.

Is nothing something?

'Nothing will come of nothing,' King Lear says to Cordelia. It would seem that everything came from nothing – whether we prefer to see the origins of the universe in God or the Big Bang, both have everything created *ex nihilo*.

One of the key questions in metaphysics is why there is something rather than nothing (if indeed there is). Actually, all something is mostly nothing, and 'nothing' only makes sense because there is something. A void or

Nothing as zero came to Europe in the Middle Ages from the Arabic mathematicians. Before that, the concept of none as a quantity didn't exist in Europe.

vacuum is only definable because elsewhere there is something.

There's a lot more nothing than we like to think. Each atom is 99.999999999999% empty space. That means that things take up 10^{14} times as much room as they would if all the 'stuff' in an atom was jammed together without the empty space. That's hard to imagine: it means that the sun, which is 1.4 million km across, would squash down to one-and-a-half hundredths of a millimetre, or 14 microns. That's about a million times as dense as a black hole. To put it another way, there is 100,000,000,000,000 times as much nothing as something in the stuff we think of as matter. And in space there is even less something (or even more nothing). It's the existence of nothing – the space within and between particles – that makes our world possible.

WHY IS THERE SOMETHING RATHER THAN NOTHING?

The existence of the universe is generally accounted for by reference to a 'first mover' or 'prime mover' from or by which everything was created from nothing. There are many supernatural explanations – myths and religions – which have a being as first mover. Physics has the Big Bang as the most likely originator of the universe, so that takes the role of prime mover. In both cases, the question 'what was before' is considered meaningless – as meaningless as asking what is north of the North Pole.

Chapter 3
What do you know?

How do you know things? And what can you be sure of?

Knowledge has had a bad press at certain points in history. In the Judaeo-Christian tradition, it was eating the fruit of the tree of knowledge that led to the fall of man. In medieval legend, the scholar Faust swaps his soul for knowledge of necromancy and the power that gives him. But without a handy apple or demon, how do most of us gain knowledge?

The blank canvas

A newborn baby can't do a lot, but acquires a large body of knowledge very quickly. Aristotle was the first to suggest that a baby is born with an empty mind, or 'unscribed tablet' on which experience writes knowledge. Around 1,300 years later, the Persian philosopher Ibn Sina (or Avicenna) used the phrase 'tabula rasa' (blank slate): '...human intellect at birth is like a *tabula rasa,* a pure potentiality that is actualized through education and comes to know.'

The baby has to learn how to crawl, then walk, how to talk, how to relate to other people. Neurologists can tell us how the baby's

brain continues to develop, how it grows neurons and connections between them, and so it is physically incapable of learning some skills before a particular stage of physical development. But does this really show the baby is learning those skills from a position of absolute ignorance?

> *'If we will attentively consider new born children, we shall have little reason to think that they bring many ideas into the world with them... [but] by degrees afterward, ideas come into their minds.'*
> John Locke, 1689

Plato and the knowledgeable soul

Plato thought not. He believed that human souls pre-exist and are allocated to a baby. In their non-incarnated forms, souls have innate knowledge and understanding and have access to the realm of forms. Once housed in a human mind and body, that pure understanding is hidden from the soul. When we learn, according to Plato, we are actually uncovering knowledge that is already there – innate. Not surprisingly, this view is known as innatism. It's as though the soul has been put into a glass cubicle with steamed-up windows and has to wipe clear spaces to see again what it could previously see clearly when it was outside the cubicle. Even then, it sees through smeary glass rather than seeing things truly. The baby, then, has a lot of knowledge locked in his or her soul, but can't access it without prompting.

Plato sought to demonstrate this by showing Socrates 'uncovering' knowledge in a slave. The slave at first seems to know nothing of a geometrical formula. By asking him questions, Socrates eventually gets the slave to state the formula, thus – he claims – showing that the slave knew it all along but needed help uncovering it. The proof is spurious, of course. Socrates' questions direct the slave, through reason, towards the right conclusion.

Later innatists often had God providing the soul with a sort of starter-pack of knowledge. Ideas that

'[The soul] is a veritable prisoner bound within his body... and that instead of investigating reality by itself and in itself it is compelled to peer through the bars of its prison.'
Plato

have been claimed to be innate include the existence of God (René Descartes), mathematical facts such as that 1+1=2 (Gottfried Leibniz) and ethical truths about what is right and wrong (Immanuel Kant). If moral knowledge were innate, it must be absolute and unchanging so what is good or bad is the same for all people in all places and at all times (see *Should we ever burn witches?* Page 172). In some cases, people might not be aware of an innate truth, but that is because it has not been awakened in them, not because they don't have it. A little nudge or prompt can bring it to the surface.

Rationalists and empiricists

Whether knowledge comes with the soul or must be garnered afresh by each new life, there are two principal possible sources. We might be able to gain knowledge through the application of reason, or through the evidence of our senses. Those, like Plato and Descartes, who believe we can arrive at knowledge just through the application of reason are called rationalists. Those, like Aristotle and Locke, who consider our senses the only reliable source of knowledge are called empiricists. Empiricists tend to take the *tabula rasa* view and assume that the infant needs to experience the world in order to learn. Rationalists allow some form of innate knowledge that can be prodded into use, or at least some innate structures for arriving at or structuring knowledge.

The Scots philosopher David Hume took the empirical view as far as possible and rejected the certainty of everything that he could not experience directly himself. This left him denying the existence of God, of all cause and effect, of all knowledge derived by reason and even, ultimately, his own identity. All he could be sure

of was that he perceived things. He could not be certain that the perceptions related to anything real 'out there'. 'I am nothing but a bundle of perceptions,' he concluded.

Can you believe your eyes?

Unless you're colour-blind, you probably feel certain of the colours of things. Say you have a red jumper. The property we call 'red' means 'reflects (or emits) red light – electromagnetic radiation with a wavelength of around 650 nanometres'.

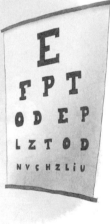

REDSHIFT

It's not only our perception that might distort how reality appears. Physics is quite happy to do it for us. When an object is moving away from an observer, the wavelength of the light reaching the observer becomes longer, moving towards the red end of the spectrum. It is a result of the Doppler effect, the same effect that makes the noise made by a vehicle speeding past seem to fall then rise. Redshift makes stars moving away from us as the universe expands look redder than they are – that is, they look redder than the light they actually emit.

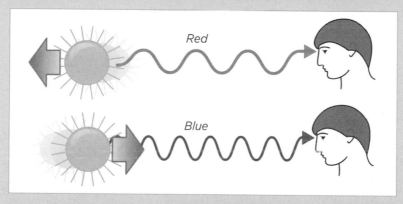

Red

Blue

If the star is stationary relative to us, it looks white. If the star is moving away from us, it looks red. If it is moving towards us, it looks blue. The 'colour' of the star depends on whether we ask the wavelength of the light as it is emitted, or the wavelength of the light as it reaches our eyes.

But although everyone might agree that your jumper is red, we have no way of telling whether I see the same thing as you see. We might experience red very differently, but never know.

Immanuel Kant maintained that we can only know the world through our sense perceptions and can't know how the impression we have of things relates to how – or if – they really are. He pointed out that if we spent our whole lives looking through a distorting lens we would never know that what we thought we saw was not reality. Interestingly, if people wear glasses that invert the image they see, after a few days their brain adjusts to the distortion and they see things the right way up, as though they were not wearing the glasses. We see what we expect to see – we can't know how that relates to reality, or if that phrase even has any meaning.

Have faith

Another possible source of knowledge is divine inspiration or being blessed with understanding through faith. St Augustine believed that he could only have full understanding through the grace of God. He put his trust in a line from the Bible: 'unless thou believe thou shalt not understand' (Isaiah 26:3). Of course, the kind of knowledge that comes with faith is not susceptible to proof. Its trustworthiness will be in doubt for people who don't share the same beliefs as the thinker.

Nativism: hard-wired for knowledge

Immanuel Kant proposed that the infant knows objects in innate ways that don't rely on a trapped knowledge with hazy memories of the realm of forms. His explanation relies on his rather complicated set of 'categories' which describe all objects, but luckily more recent accounts of nativism – the idea that we are somehow primed for knowledge – are easier to understand and grounded in something more concrete.

Modern philosophers with an interest in psychology, such as Noam Chomsky and Jerry Fodor, argue that the structure of the brain is primed to accept or structure knowledge in certain ways.

It is not that the baby already knows things, but the baby already knows *how* to know things. It's a bit like having a pre-formatted hard drive – it has all the structures set up to accept the data, and now you just need to fill it.

Chomsky points to underlying similarities in linguistic

structures to support his argument that language-learning is something the brain is pre-prepared for, but there are other types of knowledge that have to be acquired early on. Children who have been excluded since infancy from human company sometimes never learn to speak, walk upright, eat cooked food or wear clothes. Chomsky feels that the same might be true about moral structures, and this is supported by the very similar moral values found in different cultures (though that could also be explained by them being the values that make communal life run smoothly).

He suspects that the structure of minds might even limit what we can know. Some questions might be beyond us because our brains are not structured in such a way that we can ever understand an answer to them, just as our eyes are not designed to see infrared or our ears to hear very low-frequency sounds. He thought some questions in philosophy might fall into that category.

NATURE AND NURTURE

The *tabula rasa*/innate knowledge debate is a central aspect of the discussion of whether we are made mostly by nature (innate or inherited characteristics) or by nurture (the environment and our upbringing). This extends to all areas of social dialogue. Is someone born homosexual or do they become homosexual? Are some people born with criminal tendencies, or is it the fault of their parents, schooling, and social conditioning?

The *tabula rasa* view would say that all we are comes from nurture. The innatist view would say that what we are is to a large degree already determined before we are born. Too firm a belief in the importance of nature in the equation can lead to dangerous political policies, including eugenics – the attempt to breed in or out certain characteristics by limiting the gene pool, achieved by restrictions on who can have children and with whom.

Chapter 4

When is a biscuit not a biscuit?

And why should you care?

How do we go about categorizing the world, and how do we know that the results we come up with are based on reality?

Jaffa Cakes have a spongy base, a blob of orange goo and a coating of chocolate. Does that make them a cake or a biscuit? In 1991, the manufacturer of Jaffa Cakes, McVities, was in dispute with HM Customs and Excise in the UK over just that question. Chocolate-coated biscuits attract VAT (value-added tax), but cakes do not, whether or not they have any chocolate on them.

How we group things

The human inclination to put things into categories is immense. We classify everything – even, it seems, biscuits and cakes. But does classification reflect divisions in reality or create artificial categories?

Aristotle attempted formal categorization more than 2,300 years ago. He believed that he was identifying categories that genuinely divided things, a position that makes him a realist. (Someone who believes categorization is entirely imposed on the classified things is a conceptualist.) Aristotle listed ten highest categories that could be used to distinguish objects (or possibly words – it's not clear whether he talked about words or the things words refer to). The

THE CASE FOR AND AGAINST JAFFA 'CAKES'

To decide, the court considered the following points:

- The name includes the word cake, but this didn't cut much ice as you can imagine.
- Jaffa Cakes are made from an egg, flour, and sugar mixture which becomes puffy and aerated on cooking, just like a real cake. The batter is thin, like cake batter, not thick like biscuit batter.
- Cakes are soft and bendy; biscuits snap. A Jaffa Cake doesn't snap, and has the texture of a sponge cake.
- When it goes stale, a Jaffa Cake goes hard like a cake. When biscuits go stale, they go soft.
- Jaffa Cakes are small, like biscuits – a bit too small for a cake.
- Jaffa Cakes are sold in packs that look more like biscuit packets than cake packets.
- Jaffa Cakes are generally displayed for sale with biscuits rather than cakes.
- Jaffa Cakes are presented as a snack to be eaten with the fingers. Cakes are more often eaten with a fork.
- The sponge part of a Jaffa Cake is a substantial part of its bulk.

Yes, this is how the British tax-payers' money is spent... It's a cake, by the way. The court decided that Jaffa Cakes had enough characteristics of cakes to be accepted as such, and, consequently, be exempt from VAT.

ten categories are: **(1) substance** (e.g. man, or horse) **(2) quantity**; **(3) quality** (e.g. white); **(4) relation** (e.g. half, double); **(5) place**; **(6) time**; **(7) being in a position** (e.g. sitting); **(8) having** (e.g. has a hat on); **(9) acting**; and **(10) being acted upon** (e.g. being cut). It's far more complicated than any list suggests. The important distinction is that one thing can't be another – so, for instance, quantity is not a type of substance or a place.

Aristotle has no 'top' category that includes everything, as to categorize is to draw distinctions between things and, logically, if everything is in a top category, there is nothing left to be outside it. The categories contain multiple subdivisions, though. We can go up or down through a system of categories to include more or fewer examples. If we had a category of dogs, for instance, we could move downwards to a category of Dalmatians or upwards to a category of land mammals. The act of categorizing requires investigating things and seeing which features they have in common and which distinguish them from other things.

Being certain – what is necessary and sufficient

To categorize and define adequately, in the traditional or classical way, we need to find properties that are necessary

and sufficient to put things into one group and not another. Classical categorization provides enough categories so that everything can be categorized. And the categories must be mutually exclusive – so if something

Grouping by species – types of animals that will breed with one another – is fairly sound, as that is a distinction innate in the animals rather than only observed by scientists.

is a bird, it can't be a fish; if it is a motorbike, it can't be a car.

Animal or vegetable?

The first large-scale, systematic attempt to categorize living things was made by the Swedish naturalist Carl Linnaeus in the eighteenth century. He worked from visible features to try to establish relationships between organisms, and developed the familiar division of organisms into kingdom, class, order, genus and species. His *Systema Naturae* was first published in 1735 and was only twelve pages long. The twelfth edition, the last overseen by Linnaeus, was 2,400 pages long and finished in 1768.

Today, phylogenetics takes a different approach, working from the DNA of organisms to establish clades – groupings depending on whether organisms share one or more characteristics of the last-known ancestor in their line of evolution. The intention is to work out how everything that has evolved came from other organisms – a sort of gigantic family tree for the whole of the natural world. It's not straightforward. Often, there is more than one way of grouping creatures depending on which features you look at.

Fuzzy tigers

The American philosophers Saul Kripke (born 1940) and Hilary Putnam (born 1926) have attempted to define categories by referring

to necessary properties which are inherent in things – rather like Locke's primary properties (see p. 34). If we were trying to define a tiger, we might say it has stripes and four legs. Although they are usual features of a tiger, they are not necessary properties, as a tiger might be albino or might have lost a leg and it would still be a tiger. To define a tiger more precisely, we might say that it must have tiger DNA. Something that doesn't have tiger DNA can't be a tiger, so tiger DNA is a necessary property. Possessing tiger DNA is not sufficient to identify a tiger, though – just the lost leg or a bit of the striped (or albino) fur would have tiger DNA, but could not be called a tiger.

Perhaps we could define a tiger by saying that it is a complete living organism with tiger DNA. That sounds better. But the more we know, the harder it gets. What about a pregnant tiger, about to give birth? It is one autonomous body, but perhaps three or four tigers. There are more microbial cells in the human body than human cells – presumably the same is true of tigers. So there is more not-tiger in a tiger than there is tiger, yet we don't refer to tigers as a colony of microbes inhabiting a structure that has tiger DNA. We are already being selective in how we view things to classify them.

There is no biological difference between a flower and a weed. You could say that a 'flower' is a plant that is pleasing to human beings. But is a daisy in the lawn a flower or a weed? Is a weed simply a flower in 'the wrong place'?

Being uncertain

Boundaries between categories are rarely clear-cut. The English friar William of Ockham, who died in 1347, maintained that all categories – even labels such as 'human' or 'tree' – are just structures we impose on reality in order to help ourselves think about the world. The Austrian philosopher and physicist Ernst Mach (1838–1916) suggested that even the laws of nature or physics that we claim to discover are just the product of

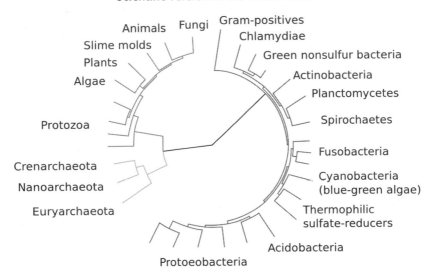

Scientific version of the Tree of Life

Animals · Fungi · Gram-positives · Chlamydiae · Slime molds · Plants · Green nonsulfur bacteria · Algae · Actinobacteria · Planctomycetes · Protozoa · Spirochaetes · Crenarchaeota · Fusobacteria · Nanoarchaeota · Cyanobacteria (blue-green algae) · Euryarchaeota · Thermophilic sulfate-reducers · Acidobacteria · Protoeobacteria

our minds, which seek to impose order on our surroundings. The laws are not 'real' – they are simply the best explanation we can come up with in any particular set of circumstances.

Who chooses?

Phylogenetics is one way of categorizing living things, and it is a way that is very useful to biologists. But is it intrinsically any more valid than grouping them by colour, size or ferocity? A scientist would say that the relationships are intrinsic – one type of animal did give rise to another through evolution, and we just need to discover the right relationship; we are not inventing it. An artist might group some types of tortoise with some types of cat as having similar patterns. Perhaps this, too, tells us something useful about the animals. Maybe they both developed this pattern for the same reason (camouflage, for instance). Or maybe there is something important in beauty. We currently prioritize science, but that doesn't mean science gives a method of categorization that is objectively 'better' or more 'true' than any other.

WHALE OF THE MOUNTAINS

If categories exist to serve us, what happens when our categorization systems give results we don't want? We have to change them. When Buddhist ethics arrived in Japan around 1,500 years ago, it brought a prohibition against eating four-footed animals. The resourceful Japanese, who liked to eat certain four-footed animals, got around the problem by reclassifying two favourites. Wild boar became *yama kujira*, 'whale of the mountains', and hare became a type of bird. Boar was said to taste like whale; the hare's ears could be considered slightly like wings – that one's pushing it a bit. By changing the category and the name, the nature of the animal was considered sufficiently changed either to salve the conscience or deceive any monks looking on.

Chapter 5

Tea or coffee

(and what that means)?

Do you choose to be the person you are, or is everything about your life pre-ordained?

Do you think you are free to choose what you do? Or is everything predestined, right down to whether you will have tea or coffee with your Jaffa Cake? Or maybe you're just a bit free...

Free will and determinism

The belief that everything is predestined, or predetermined, is called determinism. It can come from a religious or spiritual position, or a scientific one. The opposite is a belief in free will – that we are entirely free to act as we choose. Because we don't know what will happen, even if it is predestined, we all feel and act as though we have free will. Indeed, the illusion of free will seems essential. Without it, we would be paralyzed by the knowledge that nothing we do can possibly make any difference to how the future will unfold, and then feel that all action is pointless.

> *'Experience tells us clearly that men believe themselves to be free simply because they are conscious of their actions and unconscious of the causes whereby these actions are determined.'*
> Baruch Spinoza, 1632–77

You don't know what's inside until you open the present – it won't change just because you open it, as what's inside is already fixed. Is the future the same?

In ancient Greece and Rome, people appealed to oracles to reveal the future or give them guidance as to how they should act. This suggests that they believed the future was mapped out, but not irrevocably so – as though there was a strong tendency for certain things to happen, but they could still intervene at least to some degree. If they didn't believe this, there would be no point in the costly business of procuring sacrifices and seeking guidance. We could see a parallel, perhaps with the person who learns they have a genetic tendency to heart disease and adopts a healthy lifestyle to minimize the risk.

On the other hand, stories such as that of Oedipus – who could not escape killing his father and marrying his mother – show humans reduced to worms wriggling on the hook of fate, impotent to change their destiny. What is the use of knowing your destiny if you can't avoid it? Oedipus is a tragic and heroic figure because he struggles. We sympathize with his terrible position, and admire the effort he makes to avoid his fate. His response demonstrates greatness of spirit as he endeavours to do what is right against all the odds. What happens may not be avoidable, but he has power over who he is, manifested in how he responds to it.

Or does he? If everything is predetermined, perhaps his futile struggle is, too. Or maybe there is a sort of halfway house here – we are like trains on a track: a train can't deviate from the track, but can

SEEN OR FORESEEN?

Theistic religions such as Christianity centre around a god who is omniscient (all-knowing). If this god can see what is going to happen, does that mean that we are not free to act as we wish – that all our actions are decided in advance? After all, if God knows you are going to eat a Jaffa Cake, can you avoid doing it? The simple answer is 'yes, you can' – God knows but does not ordain it. If you were going to change your mind and not eat a Jaffa Cake, God would see that instead. The philosopher Boethius (c.AD480–524/5) did a good job of explaining the difference between predestination and foreseeing. Because God exists outside time, he can see everything in an eternal present. His seeing it does not cause it to happen, any more than the sun rising causes those events. God can also see whether things happen by necessity or by free choice. The sun rises by necessity: it must do that, it follows the laws of physics, there is no choice involved. But a person walking has chosen to walk and you only see them walking because they have freely chosen to do so. Some gods can do more than foresee, though. Muslims believe that everything happens by the will of Allah. This means you don't have to be particularly careful, as if Allah wants you to live to see another day you'll be fine. And if your time is up, no amount of wearing a hard hat and a seatbelt will help. In this case, your fate is predestined.

go quickly or slowly, and can transport goods or passengers.

Free will to sin?

In the context of a religion that sees some people saved and some damned, the issue of free will is very important. After all, if your destiny is already mapped out for you, what's the point in following the rules? It won't make any difference.

Calvinism, a branch of Christianity rooted in the teachings of John Calvin (1509–64), takes just that position. It states that the saved/not-saved state of each person is predetermined. This is the doctrine of election. Everyone is born completely sinful and is incapable of redemption except through the grace of God. God has already chosen the elect, selected from all eternity, and there is nothing we can do to change our fate. Being one of the elect is not dependent on the acts or thoughts of the individual, but on criteria known only to God. It's not clear whether God might select on the basis of fore-knowledge about how people will choose to behave. Islam has the same problem: only those who turn towards Allah will be guided, but Allah chooses who will turn towards him: 'Whomsoever it is God's will to guide he expands his bosom unto al-islam, and whomsoever it is his will to send astray he makes his bosom closed and narrow.' (Qur'an, 6:125)

It would seem that if God has chosen the elect, and they have

been chosen for all eternity, we might as well be really self-indulgent – after all, it's not going to make any difference. But Calvinists are always on the look out for a sign that they are amongst the elect. The elect will turn towards God, and the Holy Spirit 'graciously causes the elect sinner to co-operate, to believe, to repent, to come freely and willingly to Christ'. A tendency to drinking, gambling and lasciviousness would be signs of non-election, then, so that keeps believers on the straight and narrow. It's an odd situation – Calvinists follow the rules in order to demonstrate that something has already happened (that God has chosen them for salvation).

Physics and free will

Modern physics holds that physical laws govern everything that happens in the universe, and the laws of physics (probably) don't change over time. This means that right down to the sub-atomic level, every action and reaction is both predictable and inevitable. We can't actually do the predicting a lot of the time, because we have

> *'All physical events are caused or determined by the sum total of all previous events.'*
> Daniel Dennett, 1984

incomplete knowledge and inadequate computing power to do so, but the physical inevitability is still there. Tracing this backwards, everything that has happened since the Big Bang was inevitable. If we replayed the last 13.8 billion years, exactly the same things would happen again.

In a physicalist universe, we are no more than matter – like all other matter, and our thoughts and intentions are the result of chemical changes in the brain. Everything we think, do and intend must also follow physical laws and be inevitable. This physical determinism robs humankind of any type of free will. Only by having recourse to some non-physical animating spirit that is not subject to scientific laws could we reclaim free will (see *Is there a ghost in the machine*? Page 73).

Freedom and chaos

Chaos theory studies the dynamics of systems that are very sensitive to starting conditions, so that a very tiny change at the outset can have a very large effect later on. Although the outcome is governed by physical laws, and so is theoretically predictable, the conditions and calculations are too complex for predictions actually to be made. Weather is a good example of a chaotic system: there are so many variables to take into account that an accurate long-range weather forecast is practically impossible even though it is theoretically possible. This has sometimes been illustrated by suggesting that the flapping of a butterfly's wings might cause a storm thousands of kilometres away.

The conceit that the flapping of a butterfly's wings could affect a weather system far away has often been used to explain chaos theory: the idea that everything is part of an incredibly complicated system.

Because chaos theory depends on the effects of changing an initial condition, it assumes that there is at any point more than one possible state. The butterfly might or might not flap its wings – the notion that there is a choice suggests that everything is not completely fixed in advance. On the other hand, because all future events are determined by each small choice, free will is defending

Where would we be if the dinosaurs had not been wiped out? In one of an infinite number of alternative universes.

THE VERY IMPORTANT BUTTERFLY

In 'A Sound of Thunder' written in 1952 by Ray Bradbury, a time traveller visiting the era of the dinosaurs inadvertently kills a butterfly. On returning to the modern world, he discovers that English spelling is not as he remembers it, and the outcome of a recent election has been reversed. The killing of the butterfly altered the course of history in unforeseeable ways.

a sticky wicket. One way out is to postulate multiple universes –
different versions of the universe that exist for all possible choices
or events that could have taken place, with a new one branching
off at infinite points – whenever you choose tea or coffee, stay in
bed late or pick one present over another, for instance.

What's your brain doing?

A neurology experiment conducted in the Max Planck Institute in
Germany in 2008 has given us new and startling insights into the
question of free will. Researchers
used an MRI scanner to measure
the brain activity of subjects who
were choosing whether to press a
button with their left or right hand.
By watching the brain's activity,
neuroscientists discovered that they
could predict the choice the subject
was going to make seven seconds
before the subject thought they had
made a decision. They said that this
suggests that our sense of choosing
is a by-product of subconscious
processes. In other words – we

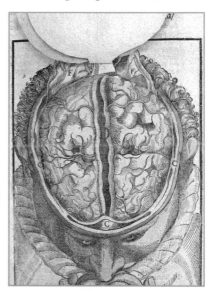

don't have free will, but our brains trick us into thinking that we do. As Spinoza said 350 years ago, 'Men believe themselves to be free simply because they are conscious of their actions and unconscious of the causes whereby these actions are determined.'

Other constraints

If we believe that we are free to act, in that our destinies have not already been irrevocably mapped out by either a deity or the laws of physics, there still remain some constraints.

We can be denied freedom of choice in many ways. A person who is in prison has constrained choices. A person who is paraplegic has constrained choices. A person living in desperate poverty has constrained choices. And we might take this further, to say that someone who has not had good opportunities in their youth or access to education has constrained choices, or that someone who is oppressed by a bullying partner, or brainwashed by an oppressive regime, has constrained choices. At which point do we say that the forces acting on a person constitute loss of free will?

If a person is destined to carry out certain acts, whether because of the chemistry of their brain or a divine plan, can we fairly hold them responsible for what they do? Or if the illusion of choice is just that, produced by our brains? Is it acceptable to punish someone for an act that was inevitable and beyond their control?

Elbow room

Of course, we can't live our lives assuming we don't have free will. For society to work, we have to cling to the belief that we are free to act. Courts of law assume that people are generally free to act and so are responsible for their actions. They don't pause to look into the metaphysical question of whether anyone is free to make a choice. Arguing from historical evidence, we can see that if people see rewards and punishments in place, they act better. But of course, they might have been destined to act like that...

Several philosophers have tried to negotiate some space for manoeuvre within the free will/determinism debate. As Dennett points out, if we surrender to determinism we will lurch towards fatalism and despair. A compromise position, called compatibilism, tries to make room for enough free will to let us get by. It depends on people acting freely, but following determined motives – so if you are a generous person, you are free to choose which charity to give to, but you will be giving to one of them. As Arthur Schopenhauer put it, 'Man can do what he wills but he cannot will what he wills.' (1839) Others have seen this wriggle-room as illusory – or worse: 'a wretched suberterfuge' (Immanuel Kant) or a 'quagmire of evasion' (William James).

Too much freedom

The existentialist philosophers of the twentieth century took a completely opposite view, giving people more freedom and responsibility than most want. In the words of Jean-Paul Sartre, we are 'condemned to be free'.

According to Sartre, our characters are defined by our acts, rather than our acts destined because of our characters. We make ourselves, starting from a clean slate. Sartre could not argue that we all have the same choices, but those we do have are freely made, even if they are made under duress. We can't say 'I had no choice', because there was always

> 'The destiny of man is placed within himself.'
> Jean-Paul Sartre, 1946

a choice, even if one of the options was unacceptable to us – to die rather than do as a gunman tells us to do, for instance. Nothing can be blamed on God (who does not exist – though we may choose to believe in him), and nothing may be blamed on any predisposition in our personalities as we have forged those ourselves through previous decisions we have taken. To shirk responsibility is self-deception.

Chapter 6

Is there a ghost in the machine?

What part of you is truly 'you'?
And what is it actually like?

'I am present to my body not merely in the way a seaman is present to his ship, but... I am tightly joined and, so to speak, mingled together with it, so much so that I make up one single thing with it.'
Descartes, *Meditations on First Philosophy* (1641)

Cultures throughout the world have supposed being human means having a body inhabited by some kind of spirit. Some have proposed a spirit with special religious significance – a fragment of the godhead or of some universal spirit, for instance. Others have meant something closer to a mind, or consciousness, that has no

supernatural element. The spirit could be eternal, or it might dissipate when the body dies, or even hang around as a ghost. Or the model might be wrong, and there is no special animating spirit.

The soul as the prisoner of the body has been a common image. In this Byzantine mosaic, the incarnate soul is a caged bird.

Dividing line

Plato believed the soul when in a body was in temporary exile from the realm of forms, trapped in a body that limits its potential. For the religious, the soul is often a prisoner in the body, yearning towards goodness or God but dragged down by the base impulses of the body to satisfy its physical

Some religions have promoted physical pain or privation to keep the flesh in order and give the spirit the best chance of attaining enlightenment or salvation.

longings. Tension between the two, with the soul always the nobler party, typically characterizes the relationship between them.

Prompted by the increasing interest in mechanics and science of the Enlightenment, René Descartes proposed that the body is a complex biological machine controlled by a spirit. This was later dubbed the 'ghost in the machine'. At first it seems quite intuitive: we know that there is a part of us that thinks, dreams, hopes, experiences, and feel that it's separate from the part that breathes or runs upstairs. This separation of ourselves into two parts – the physical and the spiritual or mental – is called dualism. But there are problems with this intuitive separation.

Mind and body

The body obviously has an impact on the mind or spirit. If we are upset, there is a physical manifestation in tears or changed breathing. If we're injured, we feel pain that might push everything else from our mind. We divide physical movements into conscious and unconscious acts, recognising a difference between our heart pumping blood and the chosen act of hugging a child. Although we know which parts of the brain and nervous system are involved in pumping blood or giving a hug, we don't know where to locate the part that makes us want to hug a child.

Descartes thought he had found the spirit in the pineal gland, a small structure buried deep within the brain. He was not the first to do this – the ancient Chinese called the pineal

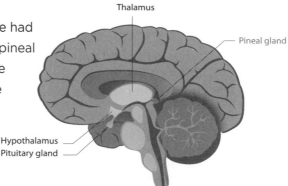

Pineal gland

Thalamus

Pineal gland

Hypothalamus
Pituitary gland

gland the Celestial Eye and in Hinduism it is the window of Brahma. Still, Descartes couldn't explain how the completely non-physical soul could have an effect on the physical body or world. This remains the problem with Cartesian dualism: how can something with no material presence possibly have a physical impact or be affected by the physical?

Soulless

Things are not necessarily true just because they seem sensible or because lots of people believe them (see *Should you rock the boat?* Page 273) So perhaps there isn't really a division between body and soul. The twentieth-century French philosopher Maurice Merleau-Ponty rejected anything like Descartes' body/soul division. Instead he saw the whole human entity as purely biological: 'I am my body.' Bertrand Russell denied the existence of a spirit or soul, saying the mind comprises simply a collection of mental events – memories, thoughts and experiences. The British philosopher Gilbert Ryle (1900–76) argued that our feeling that there is a division between mind and body comes about only because of the way we use language to describe the physical and spiritual separately.

The American philosopher Daniel Dennett argues that there is nothing special about the mind, nothing separate from the body. Instead, he sees all aspects of character, thought, personality and

consciousness to be effects of neurology, entirely determined and created by the biochemistry of the brain and body. If there is nothing special about the mind that makes it different from the body, that suggests there is nothing special about humans that distinguishes us from other animals. But Dennett (above) takes it further and says there is nothing special about living beings at all – a computer that seems intelligent is, according to Dennett, actually intelligent. So he sees a ghost in a literal machine – though of course it is not a ghost, it is just an artefact.

Brains are conscious like water is wet

The American philosopher John Searle sees consciousness as an 'emergent property' – something which develops when enough neurons get together. An emergent property is something which can only be detected when a lot of something is together. The wetness of water is an emergent property – a single molecule of water is not wet, but water en masse is wet. Similarly, a single neuron is probably not conscious, but a group of them produces consciousness. Searle considers consciousness entirely a physical effect, produced by the neurochemistry of the brain, and not remotely mystical or 'other'.

Where does it start?

Whether we take a neurological or a spiritual view of the conscious, thinking part of being human, there is a question of where it comes from and when it starts. Many religions have a mythology to account for this, with the soul entering the body at birth or perhaps at some point before birth.

And for humans, which we know attain a high level of consciousness, when in the development of the individual does it emerge? This is a more pressing question than it might at first appear, since any theoretical answer should inform our views on how the pre-born are treated, including testing, medical procedures and, most obviously, abortion.

Three weeks after fertilization of the human egg, the embryo's brain and spinal cord begin to develop. This is the point at which, if consciousness is an emergent property of neural activity, the new human could begin to be conscious. Babies born at around 22 weeks of gestation occasionally survive, so perhaps that sets an upper limit on the development of consciousness.

It's not only the development of the individual human that poses a tricky question. If a spirit or consciousness is not human and special, we must ask when in evolution it might spring into being. How many neurons have to be present for consciousness to start? We might assume there are gradations of consciousness. Perhaps other mammals can feel pleasure or anticipation, but few people imagine,

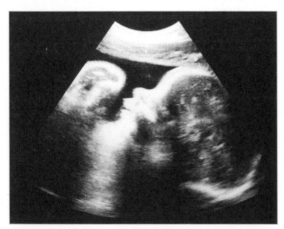

say, impala or alligators pondering the nature of evil, wondering whether there is an afterlife, or developing differential calculus. (Not that we have any evidence that they don't, of course; see *Does a dog have a soul?* Page 136).

HAVING A SOUL CAN SAVE YOUR LIFE

In many societies, consciousness brings with it entitlements and responsibilities. In medical care, evidence of consciousness in a patient is sufficient reason to keep him or her alive with artificial help. In some jurisdictions, people who commit crimes while asleep are not considered responsible for their actions.

The spirit can go AWOL, too. Madness has been seen in the past as a disorder of the soul, or the presence of a demon – or the opposite: when it produces religious frenzy, it is deemed very special. Current legal practice often allows a claim of diminished responsibility if mental illness clouds someone's judgment.

Chapter 7

Who do you think you are?

Are you defined by your genes or your job? Is there even any stable thing that is identity?

'You're not the man/woman I married' has long been a preamble to suggesting divorce. 'He's not half the man he used to be,' can be said of someone who's wasted by illness, or just by the wimpishness of middle age. Are we who we were? And who were we anyway, whenever 'were' happened? What is the thing we call 'I'?

Bones and boats

The human body is made up of cells of different types. These don't last the 80–100 years you might hope your body will carry on trundling around – they wear out and are replaced, some of them very frequently. Indeed, you lose millions of cells every second. The cells lining your gut take a real battering, as they're bathed in acid and bombarded by semi-digested food all the time: a colon cell lasts only about four days. Some cells last a lot longer. Cells on the outside of the gut, away from all that acid, can last up to sixteen years. And there are a few cells that, once they're gone, are gone for good. Neurons in most areas of the brain are never replaced, so it's not a good idea to kill them off with drinking binges. But these are rare exceptions – very, very little of you is the 'you' that came out of your mother's body.

The first-century Greek historian and essayist Plutarch tackled the issue of change and permanence through the paradox of Theseus's ship. As parts of the ship wore out, they were replaced with identical new parts. If the mast broke, a new mast was fitted. If the sails tore, new sails were stitched, and so on. Eventually, none of the original parts remained. Was it still the same ship? If someone had made a second ship using all the replacement parts, but while the first ship was new and functional, we would never consider that the second ship was one and the same as the first (co-existing ship). Two things can't be the same thing. Somehow, the slow replacement of the components makes the question meaningful. If the repaired ship is not the same ship as the original, when did it stop being the same?

Mind and time

We don't usually think of ourselves as only a collection of body tissues made up of

> '[The self is] that conscious thinking thing, (whatever substance, made up of whether spiritual, or material, simple, or compounded, it matters not) which is sensible, or conscious of pleasure and pain, capable of happiness or misery, and so is concerned for itself, as far as that consciousness extends.'
> John Locke, 1689

cells. Most of us consider our identity to be something else – something nebulous, perhaps spiritual, to do with consciousness or even a soul (see *Is there a ghost in the machine?* Page 73) – something that is the 'self'.

The English philosopher John Locke (1632–1704) sited identity entirely in the thinking mind that endures through time and is aware of itself. He believed the mind of the newborn was a *tabula rasa*, or blank slate, on which experience writes identity and knowledge as we grow (see *What do you know?* Page 38).

This seems to make sense, as we can conceive of still existing as the same 'self' even if we had a horrible accident

ALL CHANGE – OR NO CHANGE?

A while before Plutarch worried about the changing ship, another dealer in paradoxes, Zeno, stated there can be no change at all. He describes the flight of an arrow released from a bow. At each moment, the arrow occupies a point in space – it is neither moving to or from that point. As the flow of time is made up of moments following one after another, but the arrow is not moving in any one of those moments, it can never move (and similarly nothing can ever change). The German philosopher of science Hans Reichenbach has suggested that the paradox comes about only if we consider space and time to be different, but if we follow Einstein's theory of general relativity in proposing a single space-time continuum, the paradox might not arise.

and somehow survived as only a brain (or mind) in an entirely prosthetic body. But the Scottish philosopher Thomas Reid (1710–96) found Locke's account too simplistic. If our identity is rooted in past experience, what happens when we forget that past experience? He devised the 'Brave Officer' argument to demonstrate his point:

'Suppose a brave officer to have been flogged when a boy at

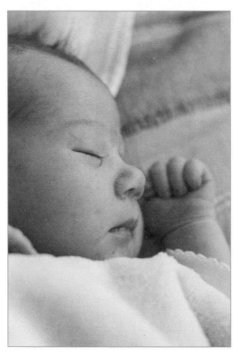

school for robbing an orchard, to have taken a standard from the enemy in his first campaign, and to have been made a general in advanced life; suppose, also, which must be admitted to be possible, that, when he took the standard, he was conscious of his having been flogged at school, and that, when made a general, he was conscious of

The idea of the infant's mind as a blank slate on which education and identity would later be formed can be traced back to Aristotle.

his taking the standard, but had absolutely lost the consciousness of his flogging.'

According to Locke, the general must be the same person as the brave officer, and the brave officer must be the same person as the boy, as the boy and the officer are linked by continuity of consciousness and the officer and the general are linked by continuity of consciousness. But as there is no psychological connection between the general and the boy, they are not the same person. Reid's argument shows the contradiction inherent in Locke's definition, because the general both is and is not the same person as the boy flogged at school.

The existentialist philosophers of the twentieth century saw the self as a work-in-progress, constantly defined and redefined by our actions. This echoes the theory in psychology that personality is influenced by past experiences, including some we have forgotten. But unlike psychologists, the existentialists didn't allow past trauma to let anyone off the hook, and rejected any suggestion that we can blame our genetic make-up or upbringing for who we turn out to be. Sartre maintained that most people had got it the wrong way round: we don't act 'in character' but act to make our characters. If you act in a selfish way, you are a selfish person – but similarly you can redefine yourself by acting unselfishly tomorrow. There is no need for continuity of consciousness, but character is cumulative, built in the chain of actions that brought you to the present moment.

Being rid of the self

We have seen that for many philosophers there is a need to locate identity somewhere apart from the body. But for the Scots philosopher David Hume the self is nothing but a bundle of perceptions – it has no unity, nor really even any existence. The whole concept of self was, to him, a fiction. Even the word 'bundle', though, suggests some oneness, some collecting together. It seems that it's impossible to talk about human beings and eradicate the self from the language we use. For Hume, the self was a sort of commonwealth of experiences, bits and pieces constantly coming in and out – like Theseus's ship but in a non-physical form. Daniel Dennett agrees with Hume that the body and its perceptions are all we have. For him, the self exists in the neural connections of the brain and nothing else – it's just a convenience that helps us to talk about ourselves.

Some Eastern philosophies see the self as an erroneous perception produced by the body and masking the reality that we are part of a larger whole. The existence of the self is, in these traditions, an illusion, and one we are best rid of as quickly as possible since it stands in the way of enlightenment.

The centre of gravity of a hoop is in the air in the middle of the hoop. Daniel Dennett considers the self to be something similar, fictional and insubstantial.

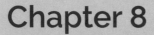

Chapter 8

Bad things happen – but why?

Why is there so much bad stuff
going on in the world?
Is the universe unfathomable
or just indifferent?

Every day the news is filled with awful things. In our own lives, we all encounter misfortune and occasionally truly terrible events. A natural response to overwhelming misfortune is to ask 'why me?' or 'why did this have to happen?' This is the thin end of the wedge. The fat end of the wedge is 'why does anything happen?' but people rarely pause to ask why good things happen.

In philosophical circles 'why bad things happen' is part of 'the problem of evil', one of the most compelling arguments against the existence of God. The basics were laid out by Epicurus in the third century BC, who asked: 'Is God willing to prevent evil, but not able? Then he is not omnipotent. Is he able, but not willing? Then he is malevolent. Is he both able and willing? Then how can there be evil?'

Why? vs. Why not?

There are, broadly speaking, two possible answers to why bad things happen:

- because of a greater purpose, or
- for no reason.

The first needs something or someone 'out there' setting the purpose. It's not very original, but let's call that purposeful something God – a supreme being with tons of power.

The second is harder to take. If life goes well, or you're good at closing your eyes to the terrors of the world, you can get by. But otherwise you might drift down the futility spiral, feeling powerless and terrified.

The greater purpose

Central to many religions is the belief that a controlling deity has some Grand Plan that – if we could only glimpse it – would explain why everything happens. Religions tend to suggest a god who is good – there wouldn't be much comfort or use in an evil god. So why then would a good god allow bad things to happen?

If God is concerned with individuals, and is benevolent, then that suggests either that there is a silver lining lurking inside even the greyest cloud, or that the things we consider to be bad are perhaps not really bad – they just seem it because we aren't seeing the bigger picture which makes everything clear. Or perhaps God is using adversity to test us or give us a chance for spiritual growth. (You might count that as a kind of silver lining.)

The Ministry of Truth version – bad is good

In George Orwell's novel *Nineteen Eighty-Four* (published in 1949), the totalitarian state has a Ministry of Truth which defines what is 'true' and what is not. 'Bad is good' could well be one of its slogans. St Augustine argued that God brings good out of evil:

'Since God is the highest good, He would not allow any evil to exist in His works, unless His omnipotence and goodness were such as to bring good even out of evil.'

This is not a robust philosophical argument as it starts with the assumption that God 'would not allow any evil to exist' and then uses that as the justification for saying that the evil therefore isn't really evil. It also looks a bit disingenuous. If we could just see things from God's point of view it would be clear to us that the bad things are not

really bad but part of a larger good. Unfortunately, we can't see from God's point of view, so we have to take it on trust, which can be hard to do.

Occasionally, well-meaning friends will make remarks such as 'we're not sent more than we can bear' in response to hearing about someone's misfortunes. (This so clearly and patently untrue that it's astonishing anyone ever says it. Have they seen the suicide figures?) It's based in the notion that someone or something is setting tests and trials, perhaps to strengthen us.

The British cleric and political theorist Thomas Malthus (1766–1834) believed that evil existed as a spur to action, prompting us to find ways to avoid or correct it: 'Evil exists in the world not to create despair, but activity.'

God's not looking

Of course, there might be a god with a grand scheme, but no interest in individual humans. The great scheme might involve – for instance – creating a race of beings which are then used for experimental purposes. Just as biologists breed strains of fruit flies to experiment in genetics, we could be part of some cosmic science experiment. In this case, there is no particular purpose to the suffering of individuals or groups – it's just something that emerges or is inflicted in the course of the experiment. Much human suffering is (collectively) our own fault and could be avoided if we put our minds to it, so it might be possible to do that within the experiment.

Alternatively, a god might not want to intervene in human affairs or might not be able to. It's possible that God set the universe working, and now it just runs itself. This view of God as something like a divine watchmaker was proposed by Isaac Newton and others. If the world runs automatically following its laws, bad things happen because they are the consequences of other things that have happened

> *'As flies to wanton boys are we to th' gods,*
> *They kill us for their sport.'*
> William Shakespeare, *King Lear*, Act IV, scene 1

– or because of a design flaw. There is no determined and specific purpose to it. The situation is much the same as if there were no god at all, as a god who can't control things isn't an answer to the question of why things happen.

Another possibility, suggested by some people who have been disillusioned by events but still hold on to the idea of a god, is that God is either indifferent to the fates of human beings or actively malevolent. There is really no good reason why this should not be true – there is as good a chance of a malevolent god as a benevolent one, even though it makes us uncomfortable to contemplate the possibility.

As few bad things happen as possible

In 1710, Gottfried Leibniz proposed a view known as optimism. Optimism in philosophical terms doesn't mean believing that each half-empty glass is half full, but means optimalism – that everything is as good as it can be. God has created the optimal world – the best world from all the many possible worlds he could have created. It's as though God has his hands tied. He'd really like to create a world with no evil, no hunger, no malaria-carrying mosquitoes, and in which hummus doesn't go fizzy if you leave it too long, but for one reason or another, he can't. So we've got this world. But we can rest assured that it couldn't be any better than it is.

This view was met with the response you would expect, and was roundly satirized by Voltaire in his novella *Candide*. It's easy to see how small evils or inconveniences might be the best alternative of a bad batch. But it's hard to see what might have been the worse alternatives to the Holocaust or the Black Death.

ENDURING THE BEST OF ALL POSSIBLE WORLDS

In Voltaire's story, the young Candide is taught by his tutor, Pangloss, that all is for the best in the best of all possible worlds. Candide suffers incredible hardship and cruelty, but always takes the view that as he is inhabiting the best of all possible worlds, there is no point in challenging his misfortune. This is 'things could always be worse' taken to extremes, and becomes a licence for apathy. At the end, Candide is a broken man with a wrecked life behind him. It's a sly lesson in how espousing the wrong philosophy can ruin your life. Voltaire wrote it as a satirical response to the theodicy of Leibniz.

It's all your fault

Some Eastern religions propose that we are all reborn again and again, with souls that are struggling towards enlightenment (see *Does a dog have a soul?* Page 136). Some of the things that happen to you in this life are the consequence of your behaviour in previous incarnations. That doesn't seem very fair, as you can't remember

the previous incarnations, and the punishment is now completely dissociated from the crime – which also means it's completely impossible to verify whether your current situation really is in line with the things you did. (Or, rather, what the being your soul was in did, as it's not really 'you' in the normal sense of the word.) The lack of transparency and impossibility of auditing such a system doesn't recommend it.

There is no reason

Democritus, writing in the fourth and fifth centuries BC, said that everything that happens is brought about by the behaviour of atoms. Quantum physics, too, says that because everything in the universe follows the laws of physics, and these have been and always will be the same, everything must be predictable if only we had the knowledge to predict it. The bad and good things that happen, then, are inevitable (see *Tea or coffee?* Page 60). Physical inevitability isn't a purpose, but it is an account of why things happen.

If everything is not inevitable, and there is no controlling deity, and you aren't having to atone for things you did in a previous incarnation, you are left with the unsettling conclusion that things happen just because they do. There is no controlling fate, no overarching justice, the world doesn't care what happens to you, life isn't fair – it's just like that.

Chapter 9

'What goes around comes around' – but does it?

Do good things really come to those who do good?

It's a comforting thought, when someone is mean to you, that 'what goes around, comes around' – that bad things will happen to those who have slighted or spited you. Is there anything to it?

The concept of karma

Do good deeds, get good karma; do evil, get bad karma. Sounds fair.

Karma has its origins in Hinduism and pre-Hindi beliefs. Its literal meaning is 'act' or 'deed' but relates to a system of actions and consequences. The general principle of karma is that if we do good deeds we will enjoy good fortune and if we do bad deeds we will suffer. It's a diffuse doctrine of cause and effect, which instead of relating one action directly to its effects has general goodness and badness spread out over time. Christianity has a similar idea in 'as ye sow, so shall ye reap' (Galatians, 6:7).

In line with Hindi beliefs about reincarnation, karma extends back into previous incarnations as well as including all your actions as a human in your current incarnation. The idea is that if you've been generally quite good – as you live now, and perhaps previously as a snail, panda, jellyfish or whatever – you will reap the rewards by having a fairly good time. The useful get-out here is that if you have been really good as a human being in the here and now, but you're suffering a terrible run of bad luck, it can be all because of your dreadful behaviour as a previous human or as a snail, panda, jellyfish, etc. There are different versions of karma. Some religions, including Hinduism, have a deity meting out karma and others make it a secular cause-and-effect doctrine.

Bad karma is a black substance that builds up in other dimensions as we live repeated lives. Only by working off our bad karma can we become enlightened. As being ill uses up bad karma, some believers don't take medicines. In Jainism, bad karma can be produced simply by thinking evil thoughts – they don't even have to be put into action.

Don't rock the boat

The nineteenth-century German philosopher Friedrich Nietzsche would have considered a belief in karma to be a 'slave religion' as it keeps people subjugated: if they act well, they can expect a reward later; if bad things happen to them, they brought it on themselves in a previous life. There is no incentive to strive to be better treated (ill treatment is even a godsend as it helps to erode the bad karma-market), and every incentive to be obedient, compliant and good.

Some other religions take the view that suffering in the present will be rewarded by bliss after death, and that those who enjoy worldly pleasures now will pay dearly for them in the afterlife. It's a similar quid-pro-quo system, but –

It's hard for us to imagine what evil actions another creature might perform that would lead, through bad karma, to suffering in a later life.

as with reincarnation – the consequences are substantially separated from the deed and not verifiable.

Quick turn-around

In folk wisdom, 'what goes around, comes around' has come to have a much more focused and short-term meaning: if we behave well towards others, we will in turn be treated well, and if we behave badly towards others, we'll come to grief sooner or later. It can be a comforting thought, and there is no doubt some truth in it. Those who persistently mistreat others are more likely to receive unsympathetic treatment in turn because we are nicer to those who are nice to us. But it's not universally true, and it's not a rule of any kind. We all know people who have behaved badly to a whole string of partners and still manage to find another, or workplace bullies who get ahead and even have friends, somehow.

We cling to the idea of fairness even when we don't find it manifested in the world. When we are suffering, 'fairness' seems to consist either in others also suffering or in ourselves enjoying better fortune later, so we try to rationalize those desires.

The Wheel of Fortune

The fifth-century Roman philosopher Boethius described the random nature of events in his *Consolation of Philosophy* by putting the allegorical figure of Fortune (always a woman) in charge of turning a giant wheel, like a fairground Ferris wheel, to which humans are strapped. Sometimes people are at the top (enjoying good fortune), but there will inevitably come a fall into misfortune – 'what goes up, must come down'.

Boethius wrote his book while in prison, explaining how he turned to philosophy in the hope of finding sense or solace in his misery. The capriciousness of Fortune became a popular trope in the Middle Ages, though it's first found in Rome in the second century BC.

Fortune's Wheel does not reward or punish people according to their deserts or prior conduct. Instead, Fortune is capricious in her elevation and then destruction of people – except

> *'Fortune is ever most friendly and alluring to those whom she strives to deceive, until she overwhelms them with grief beyond bearing, by deserting them when least expected. ... Are you trying to stay the force of her turning wheel? Ah! dull-witted mortal, if Fortune begin to stay still, she is no longer Fortune.'*
> Boethius, AD524

> *'Philosophers say that Fortune is insane and blind and stupid, and they teach that she stands on a rolling, spherical rock: they affirm that, wherever chance pushes that rock, Fortuna falls in that direction. They repeat that she is blind for this reason: that she does not see where she's heading; they say she's insane, because she is cruel, flaky and unstable; stupid, because she can't distinguish between the worthy and the unworthy.'*
> Pacuvius, 220–130BC

that the pattern of a turning wheel means that those who are at the top will always fall down and those at the bottom will always rise. It might appear that simple observation proves this wrong. What of the person who seems to have good fortune for their entire life? We can only judge when their life has ended, and since they have died then, they have suffered the ultimate misfortune, so that endorses the pattern. And if a miserable wretch never achieves good fortune? Clearly he would have done if he had lived longer, but he ended in a downturn. He'll probably be rewarded in heaven. Fortune can spin the wheel as quickly or slowly as she likes.

Who turns the wheel?

Anyone who believes in an interventionist god has someone who could be doling out the rewards and punishments required by a karmic view. But without a god taking an interest, we are thrown back

either on the normal cause-and-effect mechanism to punish those who behave badly and reward those who act well, or some kind of spiritual balancing act along the lines of the original Hindu karma. This took no special notice of humans and their dealings, but is perhaps best thought of in terms of something like the water cycle –

IT'S ABSURD

The philosophical notion of absurdism relates to the human search for meaning in the face of an ultimately meaningless universe. It developed from the work of the Swedish philosopher Søren Kierkegaard and the French existentialist Albert Camus (right). It takes a position entirely contrary to that of karma or Fortune's Wheel in allowing no pattern at all in what happens to us beyond physical cause and effect. So if you are generous to old people and kind to your neighbours, you're just as likely to get cancer or fall off a cliff as if you stole from the elderly and spent your weekends shoplifting. Why, then, be good? Perhaps because it will make you happy...

perpetual, natural and uninterested in its impact on individuals.

Or we can take the view that there is no pattern. Outside the limited arena of human interactions, there is little in terms of cause and effect. Of course, there are reckless and cautious acts, which can affect our chances of good or bad outcomes, but no one can guarantee their fortune. You can develop cancer, have an accident, or lose a loved one at any point and through no fault of your own. You can suffer all three of those events in a year – or never. Similarly, you could fall in love, win the lottery and be nominated for a Nobel Prize all in the same year.

Chapter 10

Will a new iPhone make you happy?

Can happiness be found in owning things?
How *can* you be happy?

What makes you happy? Lying on a beach with a cocktail? Playing music? Or helping other people? The pursuit of happiness is a perennial human goal. But what will make us happy, and how can we get it?

Before we get any further, we need to be clear about what we mean by happiness. In philosophy, there are two broad strands: happiness can mean well-being, a life that is well-lived (in the view

ASK YOURSELF

• Abigail works for a disaster charity. She spends her days helping piece back together the lives of people who have lost everything. She lives in poor conditions and often goes to bed exhausted and traumatized by what she has seen. But her work saves lives. She considers she is living well and would not change what she does.

• Francine likes to watch reality TV shows. She lies on the sofa, watching TV and eating doughnuts, which are her favourite food. She has enough money to do this as often as she likes. She is never hungry, she never has to work, she never thinks about the hardships other people suffer and she goes to bed content each night.

Who is happy? Who has a good life?

of the one living it), or it can be a state of mind. They are not always coincident, in that living a good life might not make you feel cheerful.

Reasons to be cheerful...

When people ask how they can be happy, they don't generally mean enjoy a quick burst of bliss, but how they can live a life that is satisfying and/or fits their idea of living well. It's quite subjective, as we all have different ideas of what that would be. A life that is full of pleasure is not necessarily the same as a life well lived.

In the land of philosophy, there are at least three ways to be happy: the hedonistic way involves having lots of pleasurable experiences; the life-satisfaction way involves being satisfied with how your life is going; the emotional-state way involves feeling affirmed or that you are flourishing emotionally.

Wine, women and song; drugs, drink and rock 'n' roll

The hedonistic view finds happiness in pleasurable experiences. It has a long history. We find it set out first in the teachings of Aristippus of Cyrene (c.435–c.35BC), and his grandson who was also called Aristippus. The Cyrenaics considered pleasure to be the only good. Their motto could have been 'make hay while the sun shines', though they would probably have found something more fun to make than hay. The Cyrenaic way was to indulge in every available pleasure whenever possible. They did bring in some measure of judgment, though – some pleasures lead almost immediately to pain, and pain is to be avoided. Even a Cyrenaic wouldn't have jumped off a high building for the fleeting pleasure of flying. On the whole, though, they valued physical pleasures above mental or spiritual pleasures, so if you wanted a good night out on the town in ancient Greece, Aristippus was your man.

> **'The pursuit of pleasure is a life fit only for beasts.'**
> Aristotle

A hundred years later, Epicurus (341–270BC) took a more measured view. It's his name that has come down to us in the adjective Epicurean to denote someone who enjoys fine dining and good living. He promoted the virtues of good food, wine, music and other sensual pleasures as a source of happiness, but not indiscriminately or to the point of all-out hedonism. An Epicurean has taste and refinement, unlike a Cyrenaic, who would be downing the vodka and kebabs and looking for an easy lay. Epicurus did not over-indulge. He found pleasure in moderation. Indeed, his personal tastes were quite modest: he drank water, ate mostly home-grown vegetables, and lived in a sort of commune with friends. This allowed them all plenty of intelligent and sympathetic conversation, and let them off having to do unpleasant work for people they didn't like in Athens – a bit of a hippy idyll, really.

Epicurus thought seriously about happiness. He considered the basic 'goods' necessary to happiness, once basic physical needs for food, shelter and health had been met, were friendship, freedom and thought (intellectual stimulation and conversation). He considered it natural but unnecessary to want fancy food, a nice house and the trappings of wealth. He considered it unnatural to want power and fame. So winning *The X-Factor* really wouldn't have made him happy.

ABOUT THAT IPHONE...

Epicurus set a test for things we believe we want. How would your life be better if you had the object? How would it be worse if you didn't have the object? Do you want an iPhone so that you can communicate with friends and use its features? Or do you want it because everyone is supposed  to want one and you'll look cool if you have it? That's not a new phenomenon. Writing in the first century BC, Lucretius complained that what people want is dictated by popular opinion rather than their own judgment. And he didn't even have an iPhone.

Can't get no satisfaction?

Another way of looking at happiness is the satisfaction of desires. That's not the same as having pleasurable experiences, although it can involve it. If you are constantly frustrated because you can't find a job you enjoy or don't have the relationship you want, you are unlikely to be happy. You

might have fleeting periods of happiness produced by hedonistic experiences, but your overall dissatisfaction will mean that you don't consider yourself generally happy. We don't all want the same things, so one person might be satisfied with a life that another would hate. To know whether you are satisfied, you have to know what you desire.

The happiness wish-list

There is another model of happiness which philosophers call the 'objective list' model. This is less personal, as it sets out the things which philosophers believe are necessary for well-being, or a good life, in all people. Epicurus's list of friends, freedom and thought is an example. He supposed these make a good life for anyone. Aristotle believed that all things yearn to fulfil their function, or do what they are best suited to doing. We might see this as realizing our personal potential. For him, what humans were good at – their function – was rational thought, so people are happiest ('live well') if they live a virtuous life of reason.

He considered that people who think they enjoy things that are bad for them – drinking too much, being lazy, and so on – are not truly happy. There is a second option for people who aren't up to much rational thinking, and that is a life of moral virtue. Aristotle considered that happiness is the only thing we desire for its own sake. We might want other things, such as wealth, friendship and health, but we want them because we believe they will make us happy.

Happiness hereafter

For the religious, there is always the promise of everlasting bliss later on even if things are not so good now. This can be a comfort in difficult times, but that's not quite the same as happiness. According to St Thomas Aquinas, only imperfect happiness is possible on Earth, but the best form of that comes from the contemplative life – from spiritual reflection and worship. We can't all manage that, at least not all the time, so there's a slightly less good option which is to live an active but good life – a life of virtue that is useful to others and pleasing to God.

DOES MONEY MAKE YOU HAPPY?

It's easy to think you'd be happier with more money, so that you could buy things you want, do what you like, work less and worry less. But various studies have shown that it's not that simple. Up to a certain point, increasing income does correspond to increasing reported happiness, but after that point it doesn't make a difference. The point is not particularly high – one study put it at $73,000 a year (£45,000), another at $161,000 (£100,000) a year. It's sufficient to meet basic needs and remove anxiety, but having enough to buy yachts and private planes doesn't make a difference. Instead, having more money than other people makes us happier. Also, dreaming of a lottery win is not the way to go: people who suddenly become richer feel happier in the short term but soon settle back to their previous level of reported happiness.

So detached you're falling off?

Is avoiding unhappiness the same thing as being happy? In times and places when life is very harsh it might seem the best to hope for. Some Eastern religions and philosophies promote a detachment which encourages us to take a step back, observe and acknowledge what happens and how we feel about it, but not let ourselves be ruled by events and feelings. The Stoics of Ancient Greece took the same view – we can't stop ourselves feeling pain or disappointment but we can limit its impact on our equilibrium. In modern parlance, this is akin to mindfulness. But if it helps to reduce the impact of negative events and feelings, it must also reduce the impact of positive effects and feelings. Perhaps whether you opt for a mindful approach depends on whether you expect good things or bad things to come your way.

'[Virtue is] a firm and constant will to bring about everything we judge to be the best and to employ all the force of our intellect in judging well... [it is] the only good, among all those we can possess, which depends entirely on our free will.

'[Happiness is] perfect contentment of mind and inner satisfaction... which is acquired by the wise without fortune's favour... We cannot ever practice any virtue—that is to say, do what our reason tells us we should do— without receiving satisfaction and pleasure from doing so.'
Descartes, 1645

Virtue makes you happy

We've seen that Aristotle saw virtuous living as the path to happiness – that could do with unpicking a little, as 'virtue' is a vague term.

Aristotle saw all types of behaviour falling on a spectrum with vice lying at the extremes at each end of the spectrum and virtue lying in the middle, at the point of moderation. Courage, for example, is the virtue that lies between cowardice and recklessness. Generosity is the favoured point between miserliness and profligacy. It's a view that plenty of philosophers have shared. 'All things in moderation,' we could say.

If we live virtuously, the theory goes, we will be protected to some extent from the vicissitudes of fortune. It's not that they won't touch us, but that our source of security and contentment lies elsewhere – within ourselves – and so is sheltered from fortune's worst effects. Arthur Schopenhauer, perhaps the most miserable of the miserable German

Children are generally much better at living in the moment and experiencing joy than adults.

philosophers, doubted that human happiness was possible but said that if it was then that was the point of life. He saw three things that contribute to human happiness and make the 'point' of life: what you are, what you have and what others think of you. The first is most important, but the second two are what most people are more concerned with. They notice too late that what you have and what others think of you weren't the point after all.

Glass half-full or half-empty?

The standard definition of an optimist is someone who considers a glass half-full; a pessimist considers the same glass half-empty. This basic approach can make a huge difference to your level of happiness, but also to how even your experience of life is. A pessimist is often cautious, expecting things not to work out and so avoiding risk. An optimist, who takes risks expecting a good outcome, is more likely to encounter the ups and downs of success and disappointment. Some people are happier with a calm life, others feeling their life is full of experience, so either way can lead to happiness.

Pessimists protect themselves from disappointment, but miss out on the pleasures of anticipation.

Chapter 11
Would you want to live forever?

We spend our whole life seeking to avoid death, but might life without an end be a much worse prospect?

Most cultures have stories of 'eternals' – humans who can live forever. Vampires are a good example. But would it really be good to live forever? What do we gain by dying?

What good is death?

Most religious and spiritual advisors recommend calm acceptance or resignation in the face of death, and preparing spiritually for a 'good death'. Why? Some elderly people, certainly, are ready for death. Many – and especially many younger people facing death – are not, and 'rag[ing] against the dying of the light', as Dylan Thomas advised, is the natural reaction. We rage against it because we still have things to do, people to love, words to say. Because we don't want to have run out of time.

The German philosopher Martin Heidegger wrote in 1927 about

> *'This is, if you like, our curse. It's the price we pay for being so damned clever. We have to live in the knowledge that the worst thing that can possibly happen, one day surely will... We each live in the shadow of a personal apocalypse.*
>
> *'[Running from death] is the foundation of human achievement: it is the wellspring of religion, the muse of philosophy, the architect of our cities, and the impulse behind the arts.'*
> Stephen Cave, British philosopher, 2012

the awareness of mortality that presses down on human consciousness. He wrote of '*Dasein*' – literally 'being there' – as the state of the individual in the world. We are, he said, defined and limited by our context in time and space. One aspect of that context is that we live for a limited span. Knowing that our time here is limited causes anxiety (*angst*) or dread. Heidegger didn't believe in a god, but even if he had done, God is irrelevant in this scheme – we still have to choose how to spend our limited time alive, and make that choice wisely as there is no second chance. Death concentrates the mind wonderfully.

The awareness of our

> *'But at my back I always hear Time's winged chariot hurrying near;*
> *And yonder all before us lie Deserts of vast eternity.'*
> Andrew Marvell (1621–78),
> 'To His Coy Mistress'

mortality forces (or should force) us to decide what is important and focus on it. Heidegger distinguished between authentic and inauthentic ways of living,

with the authentic being a life lived according to our own values and choices. We could just be pushed about by circumstances, and that would be an inauthentic life – though as we would have chosen the path of least resistance, that too is a sort of authenticity in a twisted way. If, like the vampire, we had all of eternity to fulfil our

ambitions, they wouldn't really be ambitions. Nothing would be meaningful as it wouldn't be chosen over anything else – there would be time for everything. It is the certain knowledge of death that gives life meaning.

'One more moment, Mr Executioner, I beg you!' – the last, desperate words of Madame de Barry, executed during the French Revolution, 1793

The message we don't want to hear

For thousands of years, magicians and scientists have sought an elixir of life, a magic potion that will restore youth or let us live forever. Today, we have a tame version in creams, pills and supplements that promise to stop the clock and keep us looking and feeling young. For those with more money than sense, cryogenics offers a way, supposedly, of preserving ourselves for future resuscitation. The quest to live forever, or at least a bit longer, is probably as old as humankind.

Many religions offer a promise of eternal life after death, and it's supposedly quite nice there. In the past, the promise of a better time in the afterlife was probably more compelling than it is now.

> Epicurus said that the fear of death is natural, but not rational:
> *'Death is nothing to us. For when we are here, death is not. And when death is here, we are gone.'*
> Epicurus

When most people endured a short life filled with pain and hard work, the idea of an afterlife that would redress the balance must have been very appealing. But isn't wanting more just greedy? We can also hope to live on through our children, or through leaving a body of work that will endure into the future. Perhaps that's the natural way to go about it.

Some people pay a large amount of money to have their body, or even just their brain, frozen after death. The idea is that when in the future there is a cure for whatever killed them, they will be defrosted and can carry on living. Would you want to live in a new world, long after your loved ones had all died? And why would people of the future bother to defrost anyone from the twenty-first century?

What good is life?

'All the labour of the ages, all the devotion, all the inspiration, all the noonday brightness of human genius, are destined to extinction in the vast death of the solar system, and the whole temple of man's achievement must inevitably be buried beneath the debris of a universe in ruins.'

Bertrand Russell

It's said that Bertrand Russell was once asked by a London cab driver 'what's it all about, then?' He possibly wasn't the best person to ask. But if we are going to die and it's all turning to dust, what use *is* life? This is the question that the Absurdists faced (see *To be or not to be?* Page 291).

There are two ways to approach the question of the purpose of life. One is to ask whether it needs a purpose at all. The other is to try to name a purpose.

> *'The mystery of human existence lies not in just staying alive, but in finding something to live for.'*
> Fyodor Dostoyevsky, 1880

We could be here all day going through possible purposes of life, but most philosophers come, one way or another, to say that we can't know if it has a purpose so let's just live it the best way we can. Camus, who said the only truly significant question in philosophy is 'why not suicide?', hit the nail on the head when he said that we really just have to get on with it without knowing.

If you feel there is a purpose to your life (perhaps through religious belief), you won't be asking the question. If you don't, you might take the most frequently given philosophical answer – to live true to yourself, to live a good life, to do what is right (see *Will a new iPhone make you happy?* Page 108). The 'good' of something is what we make of it.

> *'Death is not an event in life: we do not live to experience death. If we take eternity to mean not infinite temporal duration but timelessness, then eternal life belongs to those who live in the present. Our life has no end in the way in which our visual field has no limits.'*
> Ludwig Wittgenstein, 1921

'The clear awareness of having been born into a losing struggle need not lead one into despair. I do not especially like the idea that one day I shall be tapped on the shoulder and informed, not that the party is over but that it is most assuredly going on - only henceforth in my absence. (It's the second of those thoughts: the edition of the newspaper that will come out on the day after I have gone, that is the more distressing.) Much more horrible, though, would be the announcement that the party was continuing forever, and that I was forbidden to leave. Whether it was a hellishly bad party or a party that was perfectly heavenly in every respect, the moment that it became eternal and compulsory would be the precise moment that it began to pall.'

Christopher Hitchens, 1949–2011

Chapter 12

Can you choose to believe in God?

Is faith a gift, or can it be chosen? If belief is not a choice, how can it be fair to reward it?

'If I saw no signs of a divinity, I would fix myself in denial. If I saw everywhere the marks of a Creator, I would repose peacefully in faith. But seeing too much to deny Him, and too little to assure me, I am in a pitiful state, and I would wish a hundred times that if a god sustains nature it would reveal Him without ambiguity.'
Blaise Pascal, *Pensées*, 1669

This chapter is not about whether God exists: that's too big a question. Or perhaps too small a question – the answer is No or Yes, but logical argument won't help you discover which is right. Reason says No; faith says Yes. The critical question is whether you can choose faith.

Pascal's wager

One of the more famous philosophical propositions is Pascal's wager. Faced with uncertainty about whether God exists he weighed up the costs and benefits of believing or not believing:

- If God does not exist, and we choose to believe in him, we live a virtuous life, lose a little time in fruitless prayer, and disappear into oblivion on death.
- If God does exist, but we choose not to believe in him, we can have a riotous time for a few years, but then lose our immortal souls to an eternity of perdition and torment.

'If you gain, you gain all; if you lose, you lose nothing.'

On balance, investing the few hours in prayers and good works is the best bet:

'I should be much more afraid of being mistaken and then finding out that Christianity is true than of being mistaken in believing it to be true.'

But is it this straightforward? Is belief actually a matter of choice? Perhaps for Pascal,

WHICH GOD ARE YOU CHOOSING?

Pascal's wager has a serious flaw, which Denis Diderot pointed out around 100 years after Pascal wrote. Pascal has to choose not only whether to believe in God, but which god to believe in. If he picks the wrong god, the hours invested in prayer will have gone to waste and he'll still be damned forever.

because he was in doubt – part believing, part not – the wager was enough to tip him over the edge and listen to the believing part of himself and silence the unbelieving part. Starting from a position of non-belief, though, is it actually possible to choose to believe?

Born into the faith

It used to be straightforward. If you lived in Europe, you were born into the Christian tradition, or perhaps into Judaism. From babyhood, you didn't question it – at least, not out loud, or not unless your career-goal was to be burned as a heretic. In times when lots of things were mysterious and had to be taken on trust, it must have

been easier to take God on board with few backward glances. There are places where that still holds. There are, and have been, people for whom the existence of God is no more in doubt than the existence of air. They no more choose to believe than you or I choose to breathe.

Forced choices

William James, the brother of the more famous Henry James, novelist, considered belief in God to be a 'forced choice' – one which we have to make, for or against, because there is no tenable intermediate position. He saw life as filled with choices, some of which are forced (have to be made) and some of which are momentous (they make an enormous difference to life). The choice, as he saw it, of whether or not to believe in God was both forced and momentous. He could see no reason why someone would choose unbelief as religion gives a person a purpose in life, a moral framework and psychological structure – plus that ever-enticing bonus of an afterlife, of course.

Reason and faith or reasons for faith?

There is a very uneasy relationship between reason and faith. Some thinkers have argued that it is entirely reasonable to believe in God and have tried to defend the existence of God through reasoned argument. It doesn't work. There is no compelling philosophically robust rational argument for the existence of God – but isn't that the whole point?

'Nor do I seek to understand that I may believe, but I believe that I may understand. For this, too, I believe, that, unless I first believe, I shall not understand.'
Anselm, 1077–78

Voltaire claims otherwise, saying belief *is* a matter of reason:
'What is faith? Is it to believe that which is evident? No. It is perfectly evident to my mind that there exists a necessary, eternal, supreme, and intelligent being. This is no matter of faith, but of reason.'

But 'it is perfectly evident to my mind' is essentially a statement of faith, whatever he says. It may be 'evident' but it is only 'reasonable' if it can be proved by reason, by rational argument. And the only purpose of a logical proof of the existence of God is to persuade those who don't have faith, or whose faith is wavering – people like Pascal! To be fair to Voltaire, he believed the universe was governed by immutable laws (what we would call the laws of physics) and that these were innately explicable even if we could not yet explain them. God fell into this category – so it was a matter of reason beyond our current capacity rather than an ineffable mystery.

Erasmus, a Dutch humanist writing in the early sixteenth century, was highly critical of the organized Church which he believed obscured religion with unnecessary rituals and regulations – he criticized the clergy for arguing all the way to Hell about how many knots to use when tying their sandals. Erasmus felt that simple, direct 'worship from the heart' was all that was required, and that it must be based in a confident recognition of God and urge to worship him. He considered belief in God to be a form of 'glorious folly' – folly precisely because it is accepted as true even if it seems counter to reason. It is beyond science, beyond reason – a simple affirmation of a directly perceived or apprehended truth. Søren Kierkegaard, too, saw belief as a 'leap of faith' and the very opposite of reason – if we could explain God, we would not need faith and then belief would be meaningless.

Can you taste tonic water?

This leaves those who don't believe with few options. Is it like the ability to taste tonic water? Some people can taste the bitterness of the quinine in it and some can't – it's a genetic difference. If you can't taste it, you never will. Is faith the same? If you don't automatically have faith, are you excluded from the kingdom of heaven (assuming there is one)? Isn't that a bit unfair? According to many religious teachings, no amount of good works and charitable thought and going through the devout motions will help without faith. And the beliefs have to be spot on. If you're a Catholic and the Protestants got it right, woe to you. If you're Sunni and the Shi'ites got it right, woe to you. And if the Polynesian shark-worshippers got it right, woe to most of us.

According to John Calvin, God has already chosen those who will be saved. According to more liberal doctrines, we can all prepare the ground for the Holy Spirit (or other appropriate bringer of faith).

Who made the choice?

The dominant modern attitude to religion, particularly in the West, is that it is a personal matter between the individual and God, perhaps with an intermediary spiritual leader. The German philosopher Friedrich Nietzsche (1844–1900) turned against religion – and particularly Christianity – declaring it a sort of communal avoidance tactic for dealing with important social issues. In his view, religions that make a virtue of subservient positions such as poverty, humility and meekness, endorse and prop up social systems that oppress the poor. He called them 'slave moralities' because they make a moral good of the characteristics that make people easy to exploit. The slaves are discouraged from rebelling against their condition because they are persuaded that the way they live is buying them favour in an afterlife that is, in Nietzsche's view, non-existent. It's a bit like spending on an insurance policy that will never pay out – you don't find out you've been conned until it's too late.

> ### THE ROAD TO DAMASCUS
>
> We aren't all born into a faith. Some who have no faith 'find' religion and some even switch religions, either because they are persuaded or inspired. George Price, an American geneticist, had an intense religious experience after feeling there were too many coincidences in his life. He believed there were more coincidences than could be explained in any way other than the divine, and converted to Christianity. Reason, in his case, led to faith.

Psychoanalyst Sigmund Freud also saw an ulterior motive, but this time it is the subconscious seeking a source of comfort and nurturing. Humans, he felt, long for a 'father figure' to 'reconcile men to the cruelty of Fate... and compensate them for the sufferings [of] civilized life'. It is not reason or faith that drives people to God, according to Nietzsche or Freud, but a need to excuse their complacency in the face of abuse or suffering. They are not prompted by faith, nor even choice, but rather grasp at the straw of religion without much thought.

For some scientists the incredible complexity of the universe leads towards rather than away from faith, if they feel it must reveal the hand of an intelligent creator.

Chapter 13

Does a dog have a soul?

Have you ever stared into the eyes of a dog and felt it just must have a soul? But does it?

What is a soul?

People with religious beliefs often view the soul as the link between the human and a deity or creator. In the Abrahamic religions, the soul is the god-like part of the human, yearning to be like or return to God, a reflection or fragment of the Holy Spirit. A non-religious view of the soul is that it's something akin to self-awareness or consciousness, or a part of a universal soul. (See *Is there a ghost in the machine?* Page 73.)

Let God choose

For the religious, God's already decided whether animals have souls. But religious texts are notoriously cryptic, leaving a lot to interpretation and often giving contradictory messages in different places. The Bible is not crystal clear on the question of whether animals have souls. This passage on the Rapture, when Christ is supposed to return to Earth and whisk away the saved, suggests that animals do have souls:

René Descartes (1596–1650) saw the body as a mechanistic device inhabited by a soul. He considered that only humans had souls; animals were empty, soulless machines.

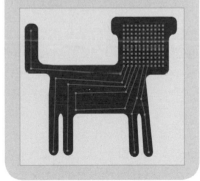

'The spirit of man that goeth upward, and the spirit of the beast that goeth downward to the earth.'

Ecclesiastes 3:21

In Islam, animals are not considered to have free will; they will not be judged on their actions and admitted to

AFTER THE RAPTURE

There are several organizations, both commercial and voluntary, offering a guarantee that they will look after the pets of Christians seized in the Rapture. These work on the premise that pets do not have souls and won't be Raptured.

heaven. So perhaps free will is a defining feature of being ensouled.

One soul, pre-used

Buddhism does not endow even humans with a unique soul, but has all creatures partaking of a universal spirit. A similar view was held by Baruch Spinoza (1632–77), who saw a single spirit of nature inhabiting all creation – a view considered heretical and for which he was barred from the Jewish faith. Buddhism and Spinoza's view give each of us, and each dog, a little fragment of the universal soul, but not a fragment with any autonomy or meaningful independent existence.

For those who believe in the transmigration of souls – that a soul inhabits one body after another – a dog does have a soul. And a soul is not species-specific: the same soul can in one life inhabit a human and in another a dog, or a pangolin, or a wasp. Writing in the fifth century BC, Herodotus reported that the ancient Egyptians thought the human soul was reborn as every type of animal, returning to human form again after 3,000 years. Some of the ancient Greek philosophers, including Plato and Pythagoras, believed that a soul inhabited a body for only a short period of time. It then rejoined a world of souls on the death of the body, until it inspired another body, either human or animal. In this scheme, a dog has exactly the same type and quality of soul as a human.

Are animals different?

The soul has often been seen as what produces consciousness, self-awareness

'Once when he was present at the beating of a puppy, he pitied it and said, "Stop, don't keep hitting him, since it is the soul of a man who is dear to me, which I recognized, when I heard it yelping."'
Xenophanes, of Pythagoras (c.570–c.475BC)

and morality, a capacity for imagination, language, empathy, abstract thought, conscience, passion, hope. Many of these attributes or capabilities have traditionally been thought to distinguish humans from other animals. If what distinguishes humans from beasts is our ownership of a soul, then what defines a soul is that it belongs to a human and not a beast. It becomes a circular argument in which it is not possible for a dog to have a soul simply by virtue of being a dog: a soul is something that dogs don't have. This clearly isn't good enough.

Increasing knowledge about animal physiology and behaviour casts doubt on age-old assumptions that there is something inherently special about the human being and the human brain (aside from any religious reason for considering humans special). We can detect intelligence and learning in other animals. Some animals act in ways that in humans would be said to show compassion, fairness and altruism – and not only to members of their own group or species. Researcher Jean Decety found that rats would free other rats from traps even if they were not rewarded for doing so – and that they would even free another rat in time for it to share a treat that the first rat could otherwise have eaten itself. Monkeys will also unlock a cage and free another monkey to share food with it. Stories of dolphins saving drowning sailors have circulated since ancient Greek times, and several human infants have been raised by wild animals.

Most people still assume that only humans create art (such as telling stories), feel remorse or guilt, fantasize, have hopes for the future or have self-awareness and a theory of mind (that is, recognize that other people have minds of their own and might not feel the same way about something). But there is no evidence either way – we don't *know* whether animals do these things. If they can do any or all of them, do they have souls?

The ensouled ark

In the Western world, dogs often have a close relationship with humans. Cats and horses enjoy the same favour to a slightly lesser degree. Yet this is nothing special about dogs (or cats or horses) – it's about us, and our attitudes towards them. We project our wishes and fancies on to the animals we favour.

ARISTOTLE'S CATALOGUE OF SOULS

Aristotle considered that fully featured souls are available only to humans. Animals can have a less rational soul. Plants can have only a bargain-basement soul.

5* soul: suitable for humans only; capable of rational thought; locomotion and perception; life-sustaining functions.

3* soul: suitable for animals; capable of locomotion and perception, and life-sustaining functions.

1* soul: suitable only for plants; no independent locomotion; basic life-sustaining functions only.

There are more intelligent animals than dogs, and other animals (including rats) also show empathetic, altruistic and sharing behaviours. If a dog has a soul, so surely does a dolphin and a gorilla. Other animals are likely, biologically, to have similar levels of the mental behaviour we associate with souls – dogs are not special. Does a polar bear have a soul? A giraffe? A walrus? An anteater?

Is there a good reason we should restrict souls to mammals? Corvids (the crow family) are intelligent, and many birds mate for life and pine if they lose their mates; perhaps birds have souls. What about fish? Insects? Amoeba? Macrophage? How low can we go?

The English philosopher William Kingdon Clifford (1845–79) thought we could go very low indeed. He could not see how evolution could make the jump from unconscious to conscious and so postulated that everything has some primitive form of consciousness that was then available for evolutionary development: 'It is impossible for anybody to point out the particular place in the line of descent where that event can be supposed to have taken place. The only thing that we can come to, if we accept the doctrine of evolution at all, is that even in the very lowest organism, even in the Amoeba which swims about in our own blood, there is something or other, inconceivably simple to us, which is of the same nature with our own consciousness.' (Clifford was smart – he anticipated Einstein's theory of relativity, writing in the 1870s about the bending of space. Unfortunately, he died at the age of 33, leaving the stage clear for Einstein.)

Does it matter?

Apart from the fuzzy feeling that believing their pet has a soul might give to some dog owners, does it matter whether animals have souls? Should it make a difference whether an animal has a soul or

A population of crows in Japan drops nuts on the road, so that the traffic crushes them. But that's not all – these birds drop them on a pedestrian crossing, and wait for a green light before collecting the pieces.

not? Just as Pythagoras asked that a puppy should not be kicked because he recognized a once-human soul in it, we might treat animals differently if we knew whether they have souls. Most people feel we have more obligations to humans than to animals, more obligations to larger, possibly intelligent animals than to – say – slugs and earwigs, and more obligations to animals

than to plants. If we knew animals had souls, would or should we treat them with more compassion and respect? Would we be willing to eat them, farm them, use them in research, keep them in zoos or even as pets?

Should we do those things? What – if any – special responsibilities do we have towards ensouled beings? Would our obligations towards animals and human beings be the same if we knew animals had souls, or were capable of something like our own levels of thought, empathy and suffering? And as we don't know, should we give them the benefit of the doubt?

Chapter 14

Can you say what you mean and mean what you say?

> '*Then you should say what you mean,*' *the March Hare went on.* '*I do,*' *Alice hastily replied;* '*at least—at least I mean what I say— that's the same thing, you know.*' '*Not the same thing a bit!*' *said the Hatter.*
>
> Lewis Carroll, *Alice's Adventures in Wonderland*, 1865

Over the last hundred years or so, philosophers have become very interested in language – in what we can say, in how words relate to their meanings and in how we can understand language as used by someone else. As all philosophical ideas must be communicated through language, the so-called 'linguistic turn' has had a big impact on what is said and how it is said, as well as giving rise to reflection on what can't be said. Does language limit what we can think, or even what exists?

That thing is only a word

The problem of universals – whether or not ideas such as 'justice', 'childhood', 'anger' and 'red' exist – is one of the first philosophical problems that brought up the thorny issue of language. Some philosophers, called nominalists, believe that these abstract concepts exist only in their name. There is no such 'thing' as anger, there is only behaviour that manifests anger and the word, 'anger'. Other philosophers, called realists, claim that anger does exist as something separate from the word – people would continue to be angry even if we didn't have a word for it. Realists are further divided into those, like Aristotle, who believe that universals exist only as long as there is an example of them and those who believe they exist anyway. So for Aristotle, if people stopped being angry – or the human race was wiped out – then 'anger' would no longer exist. For Plato – an idealist – anger exists with or without people being angry as there is a 'form' (an ideal) for 'anger'.

What do words mean?

The question of how words accrue meaning interested the twentieth-century German philosopher Ludwig Wittgenstein. For him, words are defined by how we use them. So if we start to use a word differently, its meaning changes. When young people began using 'cool' to mean something other than 'not very warm', the meaning of the word changed to match its new use. This represented a reversal for Wittgenstein, whose first work on language said that we must use language to make pictures or models of the world, which we can only do if the meaning of words is fixed in relation to things in the world.

His later thinking centred around 'language games' in which people taking part in any discourse have to work out the meanings of the words as they are used.

Stepping further back from Wittgenstein's dilemma, is there any correspondence between a word and its meaning, or is each word just a rather arbitrary sound to which we have assigned a meaning? Is there any good reason, for instance, why 'dog' should mean a canine mammal and not, say, an icicle or a carburettor? While there are logical relationships between words – ice and icicle, for example – only with a few onomatopoeic words is there any meaningful correspondence between word and thing, or signifier and signified as linguistic philosophers term them. Ferdinand de Saussure, who coined the terms, saw the spoken word as the signifier, deeming the written word to be at another remove: the sound we associate with the letter 't' is the signified and the letter 't' is a signifier for it. The sound 't' is then itself part of a sound pattern that we think of as a word, and the word is a signifier that we interpret as meaning something (the concept or thing that is signified). The word 'tree' does not mean 'tree' in any absolute sense, but by general consensus we agree to understand the concept 'tree' when we see or hear the word – as long as we know it is a word in English, of course.

Bring your baggage

Words come with lots of cultural baggage. This accumulates and changes over time and can even change the meaning of written communications retrospectively. Mention the name 'Adolf' and most people will think of Hitler. If you were going to write a story and called the central character Adolf, readers would bring certain expectations to the story which you could either endorse or frustrate by the way you developed Adolf's character. The word 'gay' was used until the mid-twentieth century to mean cheerful and perhaps a little flighty, but now its primary meaning is 'homosexual'. No one can use the word in its original sense without the later sense colouring it. This works even retrospectively, so that reading a novel written in 1920 the modern meaning of the word affects our reception of the book.

The twentieth-century British philosopher John Austin divided 'speech acts' (things that can be done with words) into three types: locutionary acts, illocutionary acts and perlocutionary acts. A locutionary act just tells us something about the world.

An illocutionary act can be a question, an instruction, a promise – it serves a special function beyond just telling us something. A perlocutionary act is language that is also a deed: saying 'I do' at a wedding performs the deed of getting you married, for instance. In order to understand how words function in these ways, everyone involved must know the cultural context in which they are used.

Do you know what I mean?

Some people see turquoise as a shade of blue and others as a shade of green. But are we sure we see it differently, or do we just use the words differently? We can't really be sure that we all see red or yellow in the same way, but we agree to call the colour of blood 'red'. Similarly, we might have different ideas of what we mean by anger, love, fear, or anything else. So what I mean when I say something is not necessarily what you understand when you hear it.

Philosophers trying to talk about language – or anything else, but most ironically when they try to talk about language – find that the means of communication is too slippery, and not really up to the task.

Not one word

It was another German philosopher, Gottlob Frege (1848–1925), who turned philosophy towards a careful consideration of language. He argued that language derives meaning only from context. If we

take a sentence such as 'That pig is black' we can see it as something like a mathematical statement with an argument, 'that pig', and a function, 'is black'. We could take out the argument and replace it with another 'this cat', for instance. But the parts only have meaning when in a context – 'is black' doesn't tell us anything on its own.

A word alone has no meaning. Saussure explained that words are given meaning by virtue of the differences between them. So 'male' requires the existence of the word 'female', and to say something 'is' a cat is also to say that it's not a dog, or a mouse, or a wallaby. In a sense, everything is defined by what it is not.

Words and truth

It seems fairly obvious that we can use language to tell the truth or to lie. Bertrand Russell went further and said a statement can also be meaningless. A sentence such as 'The King of France is bald' is neither true nor false as there is no king of France. If we said it was false, that would imply that the king of France is not bald (but does exist). Then there can be totally perplexing statements, such as 'Everything I say is a lie', which if true is false, and if false is true.

Limiting thought

Language limits what we can say – but does it limit, constrain or structure what we can think? There is an argument that it can. In Chinese, for example, when talking about a number of things, it's necessary to use a 'measure word' between the number and the object counted. So 'three maps' would effectively be 'three flat-things-that-are-maps'. The requirement to group things by one of their properties forges links between things and foregrounds one property over another. There is, in Chinese, more similarity between three maps and three stamps than between three maps and three gorillas. In English, the language doesn't reflect the fact that stamps are more like maps than like gorillas. We aren't forced to think about what things are like in order to count them.

There are more famous examples of how language might limit or expand thought and expression. The language of the Pirahã in Brazil has no number-words and no colour-words. The people have concepts of a single thing, a small group of things and a large group of things, but no ordinal numbers. Colour is communicated through simile – so red things are 'blood-like'. The Pirahã have been found

incapable of copying patterns that include several elements and incapable of learning to count, unless taught as young children. The Pirahã provide some of the strongest evidence of linguistic determinism – the idea that what we can know or think is limited by what our language allows us to say.

Some languages have words for things that others don't. In Japanese, the word 'tsundoku' is the act of leaving a book unread after buying it. Although there isn't a word for that in English, the English also leave books unread. Do they think differently about the act, as there is no word for it? Is it more furtive, or perhaps easier to condone, because there is no word? Although not having a single word matters, it's still possible to say in English that you have bought a book and not read it. What about something we

> '*Whereof one cannot speak, thereof one must be silent.*'
> Ludwig Wittgenstein, 1921

don't have a word for and so disregard? We don't have a word for the way that a worm tunnels through the soil. We could describe the way it moves, involving muscular activity that we can't do with a human body and don't have a word for. It's hard to imagine being a worm. Maybe one reason is that we don't have a word for what worms do. Or maybe we don't have a word for it because it's hard to imagine.

Languages – the same but different

Noam Chomsky has studied languages and the way they are learned. He suggests that all languages share some features of syntax (structure) and that our brains are hard-wired to learn languages using these patterns. It's as if the brain has a structure in place and just needs it to be populated with a language. Chomsky argues that any language is too complex for a child to pick up just by copying the people around and that this indicates we have an innate language capability. But the potential to learn seems to be time-limited. Children who do not learn a language before puberty are unlikely ever to learn one. Some linguistics experts argue that there is a critical period during which language can be learned and if children are not exposed to a language during this period they are never capable of learning one. It seems that if the part of the brain that enables us to decode languages – to match meanings to a pattern of sounds – is not used in the early years, it will never work.

LANGUAGE WITHOUT WORDS

No one would suppose that small children, or deaf and dumb people, are incapable of thought even though they cannot use language in the same way as adults who can speak and hear use language. 'Language' need not consist in spoken or written words. Some languages (Sanskrit, for instance) have only a written form. Some have only a spoken form. The Pirahã language (again) can be 'spoken' entirely in whistles, because it has only 13 distinct sounds and these can be replaced by whistle tones. And what about infograms?

They communicate information without using words or established pictograms. Sign languages map visible movements to words, and the sign language developed for Helen Keller (left) by her carer was based on movements that are felt. The possible forms of language extend far beyond speaking and writing.

WILD THINGS

Throughout history there have been accounts of children abandoned or stolen and brought up by wild animals, often wolves. On occasion, these feral children have been recovered and brought into human society. Studies show that they have difficulty acquiring human language if not exposed to it early on in life, but might be able to communicate with their animal carers. One of the more bizarre cases of a feral child is the Russian 'bird-boy'. He was kept by his mother in an aviary with birds, and she never spoke to him. When discovered at the age of seven, he communicated by chirping and flapping his arms.

A comparison of two feral children, Genie and Isabelle, suggested that the cut-off point lies somewhere between six and thirteen years. Genie, kept from all human contact until thirteen, was never able to learn human language, whereas Isabelle, who was rescued at the age of six from isolation, did learn to speak.

The Children Crossing sign shows stylized children – it's fairly easy to work out what it means even if you've never seen it before. The No Entry sign tells us something, but does not depict anything literally. It requires 'reading' (= decoding) in a different way – it is as arbitrary as a word, and needs to be learned.

PART 2:

DEED

Chapter 15

How do you decide what to do?

The practical applications of philosophy are in deciding how to act. How can it help?

Although philosophy is a thinking activity, its value for most people lies in how it affects what they do in their daily lives, from which way they vote to whether they carry an organ donor card and how much they give to charity.

Making decisions

Søren Kierkegaard saw the whole of life consisting of making choices, and the human dilemma in not knowing how to choose: 'What I really lack is to be clear in my mind what I am to do,' he said.

Some decisions are purely practical and have no philosophical dimension. Whether you will go to bed or stay up late to watch a movie might depend on whether you need to get up early to go to work. But many decisions contain an ethical component – something that makes one choice morally better or worse than another. Philosophy can help you with any decision that involves the possibility of a morally right or wrong choice.

How can you go about making the right moral choices?

> **MORALS AND ETHICS**
>
> There is no substantial difference between the terms morals and ethics, though some philosophers distinguish between them. Both come from the same etymological root and they are often used interchangeably. 'Ethics' is more commonly used in theoretical contexts (such as 'ethics committee').

Follow the rules

We are surrounded by rules and regulations, including the laws of the land, religious rules, social rules and conventions, professional codes of practice, and rules set out by a landlord, parent, school, employer or other figure of authority or power. Some rules carry more weight than others. If we break the law, we can expect a judicial punishment, but if we violate social norms we might just attract disapproval. But don't underestimate the power of convention and tradition: a mother who failed to take her daughter to the foot-binder in sixteenth-century China would find she had an unmarriageable burden on her hands twenty years later (albeit one who could walk). We can be tyrannized by rules that have no legal force.

Religious rules are the only ones that claim specifically to be concerned with living

For some people, even simple pleasures involve a moral component. If they feel that self-indulgence is morally wrong, or that the capitalist structure underlying modern life is exploitative, even going to the cinema becomes a moral act.

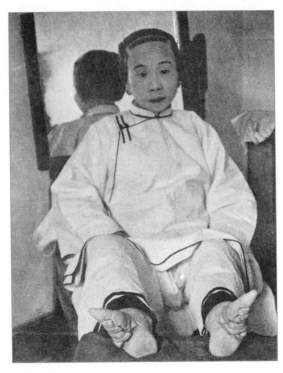

Social pressure can lead people to make a decision that to others is clearly morally wrong – such as crippling girl children. These errors are easier to see with hindsight than when they are happening around us.

a morally good life. They form 'value frameworks' which offer believers a short-cut to the right choice. If your religion tells you not to eat pork, or not to lie, those are quite clear guidelines and you don't need to think hard about whether to do either of those things. How good or bad an act is can be determined by comparing it with the set of rules. Judging the morality of an action by reference to a set of rules or a sense of duty is called 'deontology', or 'deontological ethics'.

Does religion have a monopoly on morality?

Religion and morality have been closely linked for thousands of years. Some people argue that without religion there is no incentive to be moral. Let's see if that stands up.

Why do religious people follow the moral law? Many religions offer a reward (such as salvation) to those who follow the rules, and might also use a punishment (such as damnation) to try to frighten people into obedience. So maybe believers follow the rules to get a reward or avoid a punishment, not because they want to be good. That doesn't sound a very moral position. Perhaps they follow the rules because they love God and want to please him. In that case, the reward and punishment are unnecessary, so why are they there? By the same token, a non-believer could want to be good to please their fellow human beings or because they

> 'Either one's motives for following the moral word of God are moral motives, or they are not. If they are, then one is already equipped with moral motivations, and the introduction of God adds nothing extra. But if they are not moral motives, then they will be motives of such a kind that they cannot appropriately motivate morality at all... we reach the conclusion that any appeal to God in this connection either adds to nothing at all, or it adds the wrong sort of thing.'
> Bernard Williams, 1972

love virtue. The humanist can be morally good without a reward or punishment, so perhaps the humanist is *more* moral than the believer. There is certainly no reason to suppose that morality is the preserve of the religious.

Religions are deontological. It is the duty of a believer to follow God's law. But there is more than one religion in the world, and they give different accounts of what is good. This means either that some (or all) religions are wrong or that what is 'right' for one person is not necessarily right for another. Of course, each believer will think his or her framework is the right one – how is an outsider to choose between them?

If you are Jewish or Muslim, you will believe it is wrong to eat pork sausages. If not, you will have to work out from your own set of personal values if you should eat them. You could consider whether you think it is right to eat meat, or whether the pigs were kept humanely (and whether you care).

Rules, schmules

In an ideal world, following the rules would be enough to lead us to the 'right' decision every time. If a moral framework has

> *'You find this curious fact, that the more intense has been the religion of any period and the more profound has been the dogmatic belief, the greater has been the cruelty and the worse has been the state of affairs... You find as you look around the world that every single bit of progress in humane feeling, every improvement in the criminal law, every step toward the dimunition of war, every step toward better treatment of the coloured races, or every mitigation of slavery, every moral progress that there has been in the world, has been consistently opposed by the organized churches of the world.'*
> Bertrand Russell, 1957

been properly constructed, it should act as a guide to doing the right thing. But that's a big 'if'. Often, rules are designed to serve the best interests of those in power – even the moral codes at the heart of the major religions. Friedrich Nietzsche considered that Christianity served a political purpose, using the spurious promise of life after death to keep the oppressed underclass obediently in their places. Some studies have found a direct correlation between crime and immoral behaviour and the presence of religion in a society, with higher crimes rates commensurate with a higher level of religious belief or practice. That suggests that rules alone don't make people behave in a moral way.

We all, at times, encounter conflicting duties or obligations or

The pansy is the symbol of free thought, the philosophical position that says people should base their thinking and decisions on reason and logic, free from bias, tradition, custom, authority and any other type of intellectual pressure.

face problems which demand we make difficult choices. Sometimes the rules we usually follow will require a course of action we feel unable to make. We might have to evaluate conflicting claims and choose the one that we consider most important or most compelling. If you follow a religion, you might not be able to see how to apply its code to a complex problem, or you might disagree with it if it doesn't seem to apply to the time and place you are living in (see *Should we ever burn witches?* Page 172).

You might seek help from a spiritual adviser, or you might be thrown back on your own resources.

You can only make difficult moral decisions if you know what you think – if you know your own values, how you

'The reality of the world today is that grounding ethics in religion is no longer adequate. This is why I am increasingly convinced that the time has come to find a way of thinking about spirituality and ethics beyond religion altogether.'
Tenzin Gyatso, 14th Dalai Lama, 2012

ASK YOURSELF

Philosophers like to use thought experiments to try out theories and rules. Try these three thought experiments to see how your own values help you to make tricky decisions.

- You are driving a car with three passengers. There has been a landslide and the road ahead is blocked. There is not time to stop before you hit the rocks in your path, but you could swerve down a side road. Unfortunately, there is a young man in the middle of the narrow road. If you take the turning you will certainly strike him. Do you turn into the narrow road, killing the man who would otherwise have lived? Or do you stay on your original course, possibly killing all four people in the car?

- You need a new shirt to go to a job interview, but you don't have much money. The only place you can afford to buy a shirt is a store that sells cheap goods. You have seen a documentary about the store and know that the shirts are made by exploited workers overseas. You don't want to endorse the poor treatment of the workers, but you need a shirt. What do you do?

- You find evidence that your country's government is horribly corrupt. You will be in danger if you reveal what you have discovered, but many people will suffer as a consequence of the corruption if you don't. Do you reveal it?

Are there right and wrong answers to these questions? Are they the same for everyone in all circumstances?

arrived at them, how you can defend them and how they fit together. There will also be times when terrible things happen. You will need a way of accommodating them into your world view and value framework, or you will need to adjust your views to take account of them.

Ways of deciding – using some 'isms'

The English philosopher Henry Sidgwick (1838–1900) found that the ways people made ethical decisions, if they were not following rules, fall into three categories: egoism, utilitarianism, and intuitionism.

Egoism, as the name suggests, is pleasing yourself – choosing the option that will bring you most pleasure and least pain, regardless of the impact it has on other people. This doesn't sound like a path to a moral life. It might sound attractive to start with, but it will probably go wrong as people won't want to be around you if you are constantly selfish.

Utilitarianism judges how moral an action is by weighing up the total pleasure and pain that it brings to all the people concerned (see

Should we rob one Peter to pay several Pauls? Page 231). An act is moral if it produces more pleasure than pain, immoral if it produces more pain than pleasure. It is quite a good starting point, but it's not infallible. It is also sometimes difficult to do the calculation and even more difficult to follow the path the calculation shows is best.

Intuitionism depends on us intuitively knowing what is right and wrong – a gut feeling, or common sense. Sidgwick felt intuitionism and utilitarianism went quite well together, as our instinctive choices often seem to depend on a feeling that something which harms people is wrong.

Ethical decisions – should, shouldn't and may

An ethical decision is one that requires you to decide what is the right or moral thing to do, or which requires you to decide to do what is right or avoid what is wrong. For example, if you find an envelope of money left on a table in a library, you probably know that you should hand it in. But then you have to decide whether you actually will hand it in. You might persuade yourself that it will never be returned to the rightful owner so you might as well keep it yourself as let someone else keep it. You might feel that anyone who leaves money lying around only has themself to blame if it's not returned to them. Or you might hand it in, regardless of what will happen to it, because you consider it wrong to keep it.

Acts can be divided into three categories for the purpose of moral judgment:

- **Things that are required** – i.e. you must do them
- **Things that are permitted** (but not required) – i.e. you may do them
- **Things that are forbidden** – i.e. you must not do them.

Some acts meet pretty universal agreement. Most people would say murder is bad, and so it falls into the category of forbidden acts – you *must not* murder people. But in a lot of cases, there is disagreement about the moral status of an act. For some people, eating some types of food is forbidden whereas for others it is permitted and is an act that has no particular moral status, good or bad. Occasionally, there can be complete disagreement between people. Some people consider the circumcision of infants and young children to be ethically required, because their faith demands it. Others will say it is permissible, and yet

Sometimes the logic of morality can look topsy-turvy. Can it be right to harm humans in the cause of protesting against harm to animals?

others say it is a violation of the body of someone who has not given permission, and so is morally wrong and should be forbidden. Arguments about ethical issues can become heated and even violent. When they are connected to religious beliefs, they can lead to wars that last centuries.

What does happen and what should happen

We all live in societies that have cultural norms, often reflected in the law. A lot of the time, we will be fairly confident that what we should do is obey the law, but sometimes this will conflict with what we feel is right. Just because something *does* happen doesn't mean it *should* happen.

Two hundred years ago, many people in the USA kept slaves. That doesn't mean slavery is or was right – but the situation only changed because enough people decided that slavery is wrong. In order for societies to make progress, someone has to want to overturn the apple cart; someone has to decide that what *does* happen is not what *should* happen. Then they go about trying to change it. If you are in the position of thinking that things should be changed, you will need a good basis for your own moral thinking so that you can explain it to others and persuade them. Before you can really decide what to do, you need to know what you think and why you think it. That's where philosophy comes in handy.

Chapter 16

Should we ever burn witches?

Are some things good or bad at different times, or in different circumstances? Or is what is right or wrong always right or wrong?

It's all very well to decide to live a moral life and do what is good – but there are some questions about the nature of morality that complicate the issue. Is what is right always the same? And why is what is good 'good' anyway?

Why is good good?

We spend a lot of effort on deciding which actions are good, but

---

BIG QUESTIONS: META-ETHICS

There are three distinct categories of ethics that philosophers consider:

- Meta-ethics concerns the over-arching questions of the nature of good and how we can distinguish between good and evil, whether what is good is good at all times and in all places, and whether 'good' even exists.
- Normative ethics concerns what people should think is good or bad – so whether jealousy is bad, giving to charity is good, and so on.
- Applied ethics concerns the application of ethics to life, governing how we should live and what we should do. It takes the principles established by normative ethics and puts them into practice. There are several branches of applied ethics. For instance, bioethics deals with issues such as whether we should use human embryos in medical research and whether we should produce genetically modified organisms.

most of us give little thought to what we mean by 'good' or 'moral'. The twentieth-century British philosopher George Moore concluded that it isn't something we can define. We all have some innate sense of what is right and what is not. He said that we don't need to approach the nature of 'good' either through science or ethics, but that it is 'a simple notion, just as "yellow" is a simple notion... you cannot explain what good is'. This might sound like a bit of a cop-out because it doesn't give us any clue as to where this feeling comes from or whether it is likely to be the same for all people.

One suggestion is that what is good is that which would seem good to an ideal observer – a hypothetical being with complete knowledge and who had an absolute command of reason. Another proposal is that what is good is that which an omniscient being (some kind of a god) would consider good. This gives rise to the 'divine command' theory – the notion that things are good or bad according to what a god has commanded. This doesn't quite answer the question, though, as it leads us to ask: has the god commanded it because it is good or is it good only because the god has commanded it? If the first, there is still a source of 'good' that lies outside this god since (s)he doesn't have any choice over what to say is good. If the second, it all looks rather arbitrary, as anything the god had commanded would be good – including stealing, or burning witches – something that looks distinctly dodgy these days.

Relying on divine command introduces another problem. Different people follow different religions – it can't be the case that all the divine beings are the ultimate arbiter of morality. Indeed, most people would say only one religion is right (their own, of course), and that's the one that has set the correct moral framework. That there are differing beliefs doesn't mean the divine command theory is wrong, but it does make it harder to deal with.

If we can't say why good is good, it's worth wondering whether it's anything at all – does 'good' even exist? This is part of the larger issue of whether universals – abstract concepts – exist at all.

Are there moral facts?

It's difficult to say whether ethics is based in anything 'true'. Most people assume that there are ways in which things in the physical world work – that there is a particular arrangement of planets in the solar system, for instance, or that the body processes sugars and fats in certain ways. There are 'out-there' truths about these matters. Is the same true of ethics? Are there any 'out-there' truths that can be discovered about how to live a moral life? Religions try to persuade us that there are. They have a moral framework laid down by a divine being who has set out what is right and that is the 'truth'.

Some philosophers say there are ideals of justice, truth, morality and so on which are independent of people and societies (and gods)

AH, BUT WHAT IS 'TRUE'?

Philosophy, naturally, also addresses the question of what we mean by 'true'. There are two significant, competing theories.

The correspondence theory of truth is that in order to be true a statement must correspond to something verifiable in the real world. This is what most people mean by 'true'. So a statement such as 'deciduous trees lose their leaves in autumn' is true. A statement such as 'deciduous trees are beautiful in autumn' is not true because some people find trees beautiful and others do not.

The coherence theory of truth is harder to explain and understand. This says that there must be a coherent system in which statements are true in relation to one another, and individual statements can only be true if they have a place in the system. In this model, quantum physics and classical physics (which have elements that contradict one another) can both be 'true' as systems. Statements in quantum theory are only true in the context of that theory. So we could say 'particles widely separated from each other can act together instantaneously' and in the context of quantum physics that is true because the system logically supports it, whether or not the system itself is a correct model of the universe.

A statement like 'Thou shalt not kill' is not true in the correspondence model. It tries to make the world conform to its idea by presenting a statement of fact: you won't kill people. If someone does then kill another person the statement becomes untrue. In the coherence version of truth, the statement 'Thou shalt not kill' could be true.

– perhaps something like the innate idea that Moore mentioned, or perhaps dwelling in some realm of ideas like Plato's world outside the cave. In this case, there is something which is 'good', and we have to discover what it is.

An alternative possibility is that there is actually no such thing as 'good' or 'bad' and any statement of the type 'killing is wrong' or 'killing is good' is untrue. These statements can still have meaning, even without being 'true'. We might take 'killing is wrong' to be prescriptive, meaning 'don't kill people', or we might take it as emotional, expressing disapproval – 'we don't like killing'. It might be better to rephrase 'killing is wrong' to show exactly what we mean: 'don't kill people', or 'we disapprove of killing people'.

One size fits all?

Is there actually any kind of genuine, universal moral code that lies behind this rule-making? Are some things always right or wrong? Would it be possible to extract a set of rules which could and should be applied in all times and places?

If there *is* some overall 'out-there' moral framework which we have to discover, then morality is absolute – it doesn't change with time and place. If there is not a single moral code, morality is relative – it varies between cultures.

This has implications for how we view and treat other people and other cultures, and is increasingly important as our societies become more multi-cultural. How far should we respect, endorse and protect the moral views of others?

All change?

In Ancient Greece it was normal to keep slaves and for adult men to have sex with young boys. These things were not considered wrong. Does that mean they were wrong but no one recognized it? Or that that type of behaviour was not wrong for

The differing treatment of women in Arab and European societies can cause tension when people from different cultures live and work together.

that society, but it is for ours? If we take an absolutist stance, either the ancient Greeks were wrong to be slave-owning pederasts or we are being unnecessarily generous to our fellow human beings in not following their example. If we take a relativist stance, it was all right for the ancient Greeks to do those things, but it's not now OK for us to do them.

BURNING THOSE WITCHES

For a believer, there is a specific intention behind God's words that should be good for all time. Religions endeavour to uncover and promote that intention. But religious texts are notoriously ambiguous, cryptic or contradictory, and countless religious wars have sprung from the different interpretations of what the rules mean.

So 'Thou shalt not suffer a witch to live' was taken literally in the seventeenth century, but is ignored now. There's also interpretation and translation to muddy the water. The Hebrew word that is translated as 'witch' (*chasapah*) could be translated as 'poisoner' – a whole different kettle of fish, and one that could have saved the lives of 40–60,000 people executed as 'witches'.

A modern court would find 'witches' innocent. But if the people who killed them genuinely believed them guilty, was the act immoral? Do moral relativism and intentionalism constitute a defence for witch-burning?

It's very difficult to step outside our own social context to see how it might be seen by others. Perhaps in two hundred years' time, our descendants will wonder that anyone ever considered it acceptable to eat animals, or to exploit the environment to the extent we do, or to have alcohol and tobacco as legal drugs. Or there might be some other objection that we can't even imagine.

'The day may come when the rest of the animal creation may acquire those rights which never could have been witholden from them but by the hand of tyranny. The French have already discovered that the blackness of the skin is no reason a human being should be abandoned without redress to the caprice of a tormentor. It may one day come to be recognized that the number of the legs, the villosity [hairiness] of the skin, or the termination of the os sacrum [tail] are reasons equally insufficient for abandoning a sensitive being to the same fate...'
Jeremy Bentham, 1789

The humanist view

The first Western philosopher to propose a form of cultural relativism was the sixteenth-century French essayist Michel de Montaigne. Writing at a time when explorers were bringing back tales of the strange ways in which people lived in newly discovered lands, Montaigne argued for tolerance:

'The laws of conscience, which we say are born of nature, are born

People who would criticize terrible working conditions in their own countries buy cheap clothes made in foreign sweatshops. Is this morally consistent? Are poor working conditions abroad acceptable because the alternative – poverty and starvation – is worse? Or is this just an argument to salve our consciences?

of custom. Each man, holding in inward veneratlon the opinions and behaviour approved and accepted around him.'
He didn't believe that all moral codes and judgments were equally valid, but that every individual should examine and reflect on the behaviour appropriate in any particular context. This humanist view gives each person the authority to decide what he or she considers

moral, as long as they reflect intelligently.

Lines in the sand

As soon as we allow different moral codes, tolerance and consideration become significant issues. Being tolerant of, and considerate towards, different views is often easy – it would be churlish and inconsiderate for a non-Muslim to disregard a Muslim colleague's observation of Ramadan, for instance. Trickier questions arise when one person's moral rules harm or infringe the rights of other people.

Outside the group that practises female genital mutilation (FGM), that behaviour is generally considered abhorrent and immoral. The view that it is acceptable in some societies might itself be considered immoral. Many leading figures in Islam have spoken against it, but the groups that practise FGM – which they prefer to call female genital

In the Middle Ages, European Crusaders slaughtered thousands of innocent non-Christians in the name of bringing them to the 'true' faith and saving them from damnation (though more accurately the Crusades were an excuse for large-scale pillage and looting). A Crusader who genuinely believed the propaganda would have felt a moral obligation to go on a Crusade and save souls.

RIGHTS RATHER THAN ACTIONS

Speaking against the French law banning the wearing of religious symbols in schools, American anti-racism activist Sharon Smith said that women opposing the ban were fighting 'state-imposed oppression' in the same way as women in Afghanistan opposing the obligation to wear the burka. The issue is not whether one is forced to wear or forbidden to wear an item, but that the choice to do one or the other has been removed.

surgery – defend their right to continue with it. At which point is someone's right to different beliefs no longer supported? Is there a difference between banning FGM in Europe and trying to stop it in countries such as Somalia and Ethiopia where it is common? Do we have a right to try to impose our morality on other cultures? Or do we, perhaps, have a moral *obligation* to try to impose our view on other cultures in some cases? (The World Health Organization passed a resolution banning FGM in 1994.)

The wearing of symbols or clothes with religious significance was banned in schools in France in 2004. Widely interpreted as a law banning Muslim headscarves (khimar), it applies also to crucifixes and turbans.

The opposite of rules

While fixed moral codes help to make life simple, they can also lead to dilemmas when the rules don't seem quite right, or don't take account of the context. The approach taken in many situations in which moral decisions have to be made officially is one called 'casuistry'. In this, each case is treated independently and reviewed in the light of all knowledge, circumstances, likely outcomes and context to reach a decision that seems right. Casuistry operates within a legal framework, but does not have to follow any set of strict moral rules. It is the approach used by medical ethics committees, for example, when deciding on courses of treatment for individual patients. Because the circumstances of each patient differ, cases that look very similar may have different outcomes.

Our instinctive responses to moral issues often make reference to context. Casuistry formalizes this. Suppose a couple with no children want state-funded IVF to enable them to have a child and a couple who already have three children also want IVF. The childless couple is likely to be prioritized. But now suppose the childless couple

'A man should be hanged only for stealing the shoes of children sent barefoot to their death in gas chambers.'
Martha Gellhorn, of the trial of Adolf Eichmann, 1962

are indigent alcoholics and the three children of the other couple all have a fatal hereditary condition. Now we might prioritize the couple with three existing children.

Just one rule

One way of approaching the question of what is right and wrong to do is to consider what you would want to happen to you. It's not infallible, as people have different priorities and preferences, but it's a good start.

Often called the Golden Rule, it has been proposed by many philosophers and religions since the time of ancient Babylon. It is a doctrine of reciprocity, meaning that it is a two-way relationship that sets out both your obligations to others and theirs to you. There are positive and negative statements of it:

• Treat others as you would like others to treat you.

• Don't treat others in ways that you would not like to be treated.

Immanuel Kant intended something similar when he said,

'Act only according to that maxim whereby you can, at the same time, will that it should become a universal law.' (1785)

Kant called his rule the 'categorical imperative'. He denied that it was the same as the Golden Rule, though, as it has no element of reciprocity – it's not to do with what *you* want and how *you* would like to be treated, but about what would be best for everyone.

Chapter 17

Does 'I didn't mean to' make a difference?

Which are the more important in judging actions:
intentions or consequences?

We have all, at some time, done something that has unintentionally hurt or upset someone else. Perhaps you have pleaded, 'but I didn't mean to', hoping that will make it a bit better. And we have all been unintentionally hurt by someone else's actions and felt them saying 'but I didn't mean to' made little or no difference. Just how much do intentions count?

Intentions and consequences

Consider this scenario: two reckless friends go out drinking and then drive home. One knocks down a woman and kills her. The other drives through a red light on an empty road and is stopped by the police. The first is imprisoned for causing death by reckless driving. The second is fined and banned from driving.

On the same day, a man has an argument with his wife. When she leaves the house, he gets into his car and follows her, then deliberately runs her over. He gets a long jail sentence for murder.

The first two drivers had the same intention – to get home quickly without spending money on a cab – but the consequences of their identical acts were very different. The third driver had a different intention – to harm his wife – but the consequences were the same as those in the first case. How should we rate intentions and consequences in deciding the morality of these acts?

Is it right that one drunk driver gets a longer sentence because he was unlucky and encountered a pedestrian (or that one gets a lighter sentence because he was lucky enough not to)? Is it right that the murderous driver gets a longer sentence than the drunk driver, even though the consequences were the same?

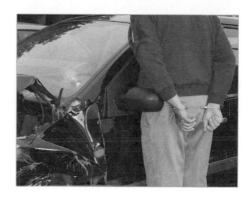

Do intentions count?

According to Immanuel Kant, the outcome of an act does not really matter as long as our intentions are good. So if a person throws himself into a river to save a drowning person, he is worthy of praise whether or not he actually saves the person. Even badly thwarted intentions still count. If someone tries to do good but inadvertently does harm, the act is a good one because the intentions were good. Similarly, if someone intends to do a bad deed but it misfires and has a beneficial outcome, the deed remains immoral.

It's all about you

Kant's is an intentionalist view – that the morality of an act begins and ends with the intentions behind it. This makes every act about

Even if one of the children chokes on the sweets, sharing them was still a good act in Kant's view.

the perpetrator and not about the person or people affected – an ideal philosophical position for the 'me' generation. Judging the act is then judging the person who carries it out. Exactly the same act can be deemed more or less morally good depending on the intentions behind it.

If we took a purely intentionalist view, both drunk drivers would be treated in the same way – either both banned, or both jailed.

Suffer the consequences

The opposite view is consequentialist – it considers the outcome (consequences) as supremely important in deciding how we judge the act. In a purely consequentialist scheme, the intention behind an act is irrelevant. In some ways this appeals to our sense of fairness. It means the drunk driver who kills someone is punished more harshly than the drunk driver who doesn't because he or she has caused more harm.

But there is more at stake here than intentions and consequences. The act of drunk-driving fits into a larger scheme of justice, retribution and deterrence. We need our legal penalties to take

SIR GOWTHER: HERO OR VILLAIN?

The medieval story of Sir Gowther tackles the intentionalist/ consequentialist dilemma head on, and throws in a consideration of free will and determinism for good measure. Sir Gowther is conceived when his mother is raped by a devil. As an infant, he carries out all kinds of heinous deeds, such as pushing nuns off cliffs and biting his wet-nurses. This is easy to account for – he is, after all, spawn of the devil. His behaviour doesn't improve as he grows older. Eventually, someone explains to Gowther that he is bad because he is demonic, so he is just acting out his fate. This greatly troubles him, as his sole ambition is to act in a shocking, perverse way. In order to be as contrary as possible, he resolves to behave well. Thereafter, he does good deeds and defies everyone's expectations. Are Gowther's deeds morally good? His intention was not to do good, but to act perversely by doing good.

account of both the actual and the *possible* consequences. Too light a penalty suggests an offence isn't serious. It leaves victims feeling undervalued and doesn't deter others from the same act. On the other hand, penalties that are too severe backfire. If everyone convicted of drunk-driving were sentenced as though they had killed someone, it would lead to other crimes – such as people fleeing

THE BLOODY CODE

During the eighteenth century, the death penalty was imposed for an ever-increasing number of crimes in Britain. By 1800, there were 220 capital crimes, including 'being in the company of Gypsies for one month', 'strong evidence of malice in a child aged 7–14 years of age' and 'using a disguise whilst committing a crime'. (Presumably the last of those attracted two death penalties – one for the disguise and one for the crime.) The penalty was intended to have a deterrent effect; as George Savile said in the seventeenth century, 'Men are not hanged for stealing horses, but that horses may not be stolen.'

the scene of even a minor accident.

The feeling that the death penalty was unfair led to a refusal to impose it. Juries began to find clearly guilty people not guilty, and sentences passed were often commuted or abandoned: of 35,000 death sentences handed down in 1770–1830, only 7,000 were carried out. Instead of passing the death penalty, courts began to impose transportation – compulsory relocation to Australia, then a British colony. The law was reformed in 1823, removing the death penalty for all crimes except murder and treason.

> **LESSONS FROM ANCIENT CHINA**
>
> In the fifth century BC, the Chinese philosopher Mozi proposed the earliest form of consequentialism. He did not pay attention to the good of individuals, but looked at the consequences of an action in terms of its effect on the whole of society. Goods to society were stable social order, sufficient wealth and increasing the population. As he lived in a time of frequent wars and famines, population growth was an important consideration if a state was to survive rather than be overrun by neighbouring states.

How do we judge the consequences?

Consequentialism begs the question of how we judge whether consequences are good or bad, and who makes that judgement. This can involve weighing up the effects on different people or groups – a utilitarian approach. There might also be long-term and short-term consequences that cast an action in different lights.

Consequences can be more or less predictable. Sometimes, it's impossible for someone to foresee the consequences of their actions. Suppose that as a small child, Adolf Hitler had fallen into a river. A passing good Samaritan saves the boy. In the short term, this is a good action with good consequences, and the child's saviour could expect praise. But with the benefit of hindsight we can say it might have been better to let little Adolf drown if the consequences of saving him included the Second World War and the Holocaust. Surely, no one can be blamed for not being able to predict the distant future?

A hard-line consequentialist will say that an act is wrong if the consequences are bad, no matter whether they could be or were foreseen by anyone – but few people would leave a child to drown on the off-chance that he might grow up to be a war criminal.

Now suppose that you buy a cheap toy for a child. It is badly made and faulty, but you don't notice. It breaks, and the child is hurt. The consequences were foreseeable – someone else might have noticed the toy was faulty, but you didn't – but they weren't foreseen or intended. Was the act morally bad? What if you did notice the toy was faulty but didn't think it would matter? Then the consequences were foreseeable and foreseen but not intended. Was it wrong to give the child the toy? Only if you had expected the child to be hurt by the toy would the consequences be foreseeable, foreseen *and* intended.

Who should be working out the likely consequences? If we leave it to each individual, we will end up with the bizarre position in which a wiser person is more culpable for their mistakes as they would be deemed better able to foresee consequences. Some philosophers suggest a hypothetical knowledgeable but impartial observer should be the judge. This is rather like the ideal juror in English law as 'the man on the Clapham omnibus' – a fairly normal person with no axe to grind, no psychosis that might lead to an odd judgment, and so on. Other philosophers say only an omniscient observer can really judge. That makes it difficult for anyone to be sure they have taken sufficient care in assessing the likely consequences of their actions.

The first position is more liberal, and therefore workable,

allowing that if someone has taken due care to discover the likely consequences, they are acting responsibly. The chance of causing an accident by driving after drinking is not particularly remote. The drunk driver is therefore negligent in ignoring the risk, the accident being foreseeable by a knowledgeable observer. The chance of a child you save from drowning growing up into a war criminal is slight and unforeseeable, so dragging Adolf from the river is still a good act.

The conclusion of consequentialism is that no act is innately right or wrong as its outcome will determine its morality. Even acts that look incontestably immoral could be right in some circumstances.

Should we just follow the rules?

Life would be tediously sluggish if we had to consider the likely and possible consequences of every act. Instead, we can use the shortcut of referring to the legal or religious rules society has put in place. This is called 'rule consequentialism'. Our rule systems are generally based on a consequentialist approach: we devise rules on the basis of what might happen in various circumstances. These expectations are derived from past experience. As drunk driving quite often has a bad outcome, it is illegal. But there are circumstances in which the rules are not a very good guide. Every country has a law against killing people – but if a gunman opened fire on a room full of school children, a teacher who killed him would be considered a hero.

Assessing each act individually is called 'act consequentialism'. The plucky teacher who kills a gunman is following this approach. As a day-to-day basis for choosing how to act, it's not very practical, as each person must assess the likely and possible outcomes of each act before doing anything. Life would be very slow and unpredictable as people would assess situations and acts differently. In some cases, the delay in deciding would itself produce a bad outcome. Someone with practical wisdom would make better choices than an inexperienced, younger or less wise person so the effectiveness would be uneven. Many people would prioritize beneficial consequences to themselves and their families, while rule consequentialism prioritizes benefits to the community as a whole or to the majority. In exceptional cases – such as the teacher facing the gunman – act consequentialism can give the best results.

A compromise position is two-level consequentialism, associated with the philosophers

R.M. Hare and Peter Singer. This combines act consequentialism and rule consequentialism. If the consequences of an act can be reliably foreseen, act consequentialism holds. If the consequences are too difficult to predict, rule consequentialism steps in.

> *'The best argument for rule-consequentialism is that it does a better job than its rivals of matching and tying together our moral convictions, as well as offering us help with our moral disagreements and uncertainties.'*
> Brad Hooker, Professor of Philosophy, University of Reading

THE ACTS AND OMISSIONS DOCTRINE

In some cases, acts and failures-to-act are seen as equivalent in moral terms. So if you could save someone by not doing something – such as revealing their whereabouts to criminals looking for them – then omitting to act is a moral act of the same type as giving them a hiding place. But in some cases, acts and omissions are treated differently. In medical ethics, for example, the same outcome – the death of a terminally ill patient – could result from withholding treatment, or turning off life-support, or putting a pillow over the patient's face. A medical ethics committee might approve either of the first two but not the third. The first is an omission, the third is an act, and the second is somewhere in between – an omission that becomes an act.

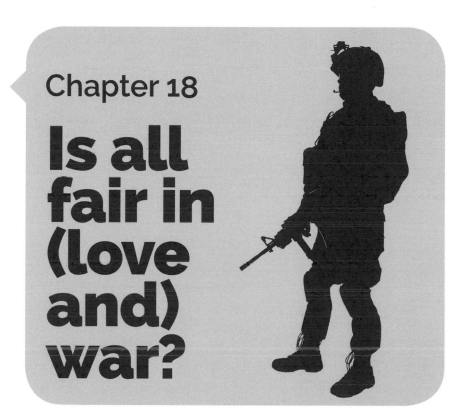

Chapter 18

Is all fair in (love and) war?

We can excuse lots of things by saying the ends justify the means – but do they really? Who is to decide whether they do?

Ends and means

The view that the morality of an action depends on its consequences is called, unsurprisingly, consequentialism (see *Does 'I didn't mean to' make a difference?* Page 187). When we talk about the ends justifying the means, the ends are the intended consequences.

Whether the ends justify the means will depend on:

- whether the ends were justifiable anyway
- whether the ends were achieved
- the means that were employed.

Suppose one state invades another with the intention of deposing a terrible dictator – and set aside for now the question of whether that state has any right to involve itself in the internal affairs of the other. If the invading state achieves its aim quickly and with no bloodshed, few will regret the action. But if the invading state killed

100,000 civilians, would the ends justify the means? What if the invading state killed 100,000 civilians and still failed to overthrow the despot? Would the ends justify the slaughter? The intention was the same, but the consequences different.

Just war?

When is war justified? It might be nice to say it's never justified, but most people would accept that if no one was prepared even to defend themselves we'd soon be overrun by land-grabbing tyrants.

The idea of justifying war is an old one. It aims to reconcile two conflicting principles:

- that it's wrong to kill people
- that states have a duty to defend their citizens and justice.

Sometimes, force and violence seem to be the only ways to defend innocent lives.

The Roman Cicero argued that the only justification for war was 'just vengeance' or self-defence. He included defence of honour, so that pushes it a bit further.

THEY SHALL NOT PERISH

He said a war could only be justified if it has been declared and if compensation for wrongs has been sought and refused, with war being the action of last resort.

St Augustine felt that war was always sinful, but also recognized that wars will always happen. He decided that they were sometimes allowable as long as they were waged to stop sin. This could mean driving back invaders, deposing cruel despots, and so on. But the term 'sin' is problematic. The Crusaders believed Muslims were sinful infidels, so if a war of religion could convert them it would be stopping sin. This clearly wouldn't be acceptable now. Every religion could make the same point – we would be forever fighting in order to prevent the 'sin' of people following the wrong religion. Augustine also allowed war as a punishment, which would not now be considered just cause. Neither Cicero nor Augustine would sanction a war waged for reasons of

> *'We do not seek peace in order to be at war, but we go to war that we may have peace. Be peaceful, therefore, in warring, so that you may vanquish those whom you war against, and bring them to the prosperity of peace.*
>
> *'A just war is wont to be described as one that avenges wrongs, when a nation or state has to be punished, for refusing to make amends for the wrongs inflicted by its subjects, or to restore what it has seized unjustly.'*
> St Augustine, fourth century

cruelty or desire to extend a state's territory.

Augustine considered a war justified if it was the lesser of two evils – if it prevented or halted a greater evil. Thomas Aquinas, 800 years later, considered the means employed in war – the '*jus in bello*'. During the sixteenth century, the principles which have become pretty much universal were established.

Judging the ends

In order to judge whether ends are good, we need a measure of 'good'. This isn't as straightforward as it sounds. On the whole, it's better to be alive than dead, better to be free than in prison (unless free people are starving and prisoners are fed). But some other things are debatable. Should we overthrow a dictator to bring democracy to a country? Who is to say democracy is a good thing?

Extraordinary measures

In times of war and emergency, different rules often operate. Soldiers are shot for deserting, looters are shot for ransacking earthquake rubble or shops left unprotected and innocent people are interrogated or imprisoned just in case they might pose a national threat. During the Second World War, Japanese residents in the USA and Italian residents in the UK were amongst those moved to internment camps even though there was no evidence to suggest they were working for the enemy. Most people felt this was the lesser of two evils – that there is less harm in imprisoning innocent people than perhaps jeopardizing a whole population. It is a utilitarian way of deciding whether the ends justify the means.

An alternative is not even to try to justify the means. Some political philosophers have argued that in war, any means are justified if the

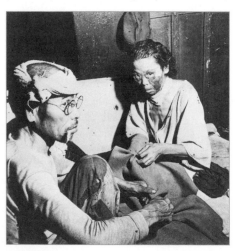

end (that is, the reason for the war) is justified. If innocent civilians have to die to secure a speedy victory, so be it. Others believe some acts are intrinsically immoral – such as bombing hospitals – and can never be justified. In practical terms, the brutality of war

Can the massive human cost of nuclear weapons be justified in any military cause?

often overtakes ethical positions. Some philosophers have taken a pragmatic view and said ethical judgments can't be applied in war. Others have gone further and said that war lies outside the scope of ethics altogether.

The dictator's viewpoint

Niccolò Machiavelli, writing for the guidance of political leaders in *The Prince*, believed the ends always justify the means as long as the ends are the right ends. For a prince (political leader) this means keeping power. Machiavelli was amoral rather than immoral. The measures he recommended are directed solely at being a successful ruler. He ruled out despotism not because it is wrong but because despots attract enemies and are likely to be overthrown.

> *'A new prince cannot escape a name for cruelty, for he who quells disorder by a few signal examples will, in the end, be the more merciful.'*
> Machiavelli, 1532

IS TORTURE EVER JUSTIFIED?

More recently, the use of 'extraordinary rendition' – whereby suspects are sent to countries where torture is allowed – and measures such as 'waterboarding' call into question the type of behaviour allowed in a war and the means that might or might not be justified in securing ends.

It's possible to make a utilitarian argument in favour of the use of torture: if it can elicit information that will protect innocent people, the harm to the tortured prisoner might be offset by the greater benefit. Arguments against torture can be pragmatic – it doesn't work – or ethical. One argument is that our own moral standing is reduced by engaging in unethical behaviours such as torture – that is, it's spiritually damaging to the perpetrator. Those in favour of using torture often call it something else, such as 'enhanced interrogation techniques'. This acknowledges that torture is considered unacceptable (and illegal under international treaties), and attempts to deflect bad publicity. Does dishonesty just compound the immorality or doesn't it make any difference what it's called?

Chapter 19

Could we make a perfect society?

Must the poor always be with us and politicians always be corrupt? Or could things be better? And how would this come about?

Most of us grumble about modern society and our own particular national and regional governments – that's nothing new. Every administration in history might have had 'could do better' written on its report card. But could any society ever do well enough?

Imagining the city

It's 2,400 years since the ancient Greek philosopher Plato wrote *The Republic* in which he examined how best to run a hypothetical state.

> '*When several villages are united in a single complete community, large enough to be nearly or quite self-sufficing, the state comes into existence, originating in the bare needs of life, and continuing in existence for the sake of a good life. And, therefore, if the earlier forms of society are natural [i.e. the family and the village], so is the state, for it is the end of them, and the nature of a thing is its end. For what each thing is when fully developed, we call its nature, whether we are speaking of a man, a horse, or a family.*'
> Aristotle, *Politics*

Plato's model had philosopher-kings in charge, with considerable constraints on what they could do. In his view, only philosophers can see the 'form' (metaphysical ideal) of justice and so they are best equipped to try to approximate it in a society. Plato wasn't a fan of democracy, considering it the second-worst form of government after tyranny.

Although tyrants might seem to enjoy a good life, Plato assures us that a tyrant 'never tastes of true freedom or friendship'.

Plato's ideal has been criticized for promoting totalitarianism. To be fair, he wrote more than two millennia before we had had any totalitarian regimes, so he couldn't have known how badly wrong it could go.

Another famous imaginary society is described in Thomas More's *Utopia* (1516). It's not clear whether he intended it as an ideal or just a satirical criticism of contemporary England. There is no private property in Utopia, and all goods are held in warehouses and handed out to people who need them. Houses are identical and households have to move every ten years to prevent them becoming too attached to one house. Each household has two slaves, who are either drawn from neighbouring countries or are Utopian criminals. Everyone dresses alike and must work on farms at regular intervals. They also learn another useful craft, and everyone who is fit must work, men and women working equally at all jobs. The ruling class of officials is drawn from those children who are identified at an early age as well-equipped to learn and then specially educated. Officials

THE IDEAL REPUBLIC

In Plato's ideal Republic, there is no discrimination between men and women, who are taught the same things and so able to perform all the same roles. There are no slaves, but otherwise there is a social hierarchy (four estates or classes of people) and social mobility is minimal. Children are raised communally without knowledge of their parents, and adults are paired off for reproduction based on genetic criteria. This eradicates family ties that can lead to nepotism and forges strong ties of loyalty to the state and the communal 'good'. The young are taught only useful things – no poetry or other unnecessary art. The ruling classes are not allowed wealth, as that can lead to corruption, but the producers may be rich or poor. The philosopher-kings are chosen from the warrior class, and subject to the most stringent restrictions. They are educated for fifty years before being called upon to rule.

only remain in post for as long as they are good at their jobs. Gold is used to make chains for criminals and so is not revered; jewels are worn by children and given up at adolescence when they are considered babyish.

There have been plenty of subsequent fictitious city states that either genuinely

'Life in More's Utopia, as in most others, would be intolerably dull. Diversity is essential to happiness, and in Utopia there is hardly any.'
Bertrand Russell, 1945

propose an ideal form of government or that satirize the authors' own inadequate society. In proposing how an ideal state should be governed, all beg the question – is a perfect society possible?

All together?

Both Plato and More took a collectivist approach – they focus on society as an organism in its own right that is more than the sum of its constituent individuals.

There are similarities between More's Utopia and Communist states such as the USSR.

It would be nice to think that what is good for society as a whole also best serves individual citizens, but it seems not to be the case. There are probably few people who would like to live in a society where their partner is chosen for them on genetic grounds and their children taken away for communal rearing, where they can't choose the décor of their homes or the clothes they wear or the job they do. These strategies aim to reduce envy, discord and disruption, and so to make a society which runs smoothly, provides sufficient for everyone's needs and is successful in itself. But it's not somewhere many of us would choose to move to.

Today, we set a lot more store by personal freedoms and choice, and expressing our individuality. Most people object to too much regulation by the state and liken it, pejoratively, to the over-regulated states of certain communist countries. Perhaps our view has changed because now – at least in the developed world – many of our basic needs are met. Our priorities have changed since Plato's time; we've become more demanding.

Even though almost all scientists now agree that climate change is caused by human activity, the world does not prioritize measures to protect us all over measures to help individuals achieve personal goals.

Why have a society at all?

If society is always in a state of tension between the requirements of the group and the requirements of the individual, why have it at all?

Aristotle believed that people naturally come together to form societies. We benefit from communal living, which gives us security, a wider variety of goods than we could gather alone, and the benefits of companionship. For this reason we are willing to exchange some freedoms for the greater benefits offered by living in a society and entering into a 'social contract'.

The seventeenth-century English philosopher Thomas Hobbes took a darker view of humankind. He felt that if we didn't live in societies, it would be everyone for him- or herself and we would be perpetually fighting one another and doing nothing gainful. Society is preferable

'In such condition [i.e. natural man, outside society] there is no place for industry, because the fruit thereof is uncertain, and consequently, no culture of the earth, no navigation, nor the use of commodities that may be imported by sea, no commodious building, no instruments of moving and removing such things as require much force, no knowledge of the face of the earth, no account of time, no arts, no letters, no society, and which is worst of all, continual fear and danger of violent death, and the life of man, solitary, poor, nasty, brutish, and short.'
Thomas Hobbes, *Leviathan*, 1651

because it means we don't have to live looking over our shoulders for someone approaching with a club. We give up natural rights in exchange for creating moral obligations in forming a social contract, but those obligations protect us.

Hobbes lists the laws of nature, though saying they can't really be called 'laws' as there is no one to enforce them. The first two are most significant: (1) every man must be considered to have a right to all things; (2) every man ought to be willing to give up that right if everyone else does the same. The reason people will wish to join a commonwealth and choose to be ruled by another or others is 'the foresight of their own preservation, and of a more contented life'. He considered that human desires are so varied that trying to build a society around trying to meet them would be impossible. Instead, he felt society could be built around avoiding the worst evil – violent death – as most people would agree that was a bad thing.

'Forced to be free'

The opposite to Hobbes' view is that humankind is more noble in the 'natural state' than when living in society. The eighteenth-century French philosopher Jean-Jacques Rousseau believed the natural human is noble-spirited and that it is the constraints of society that bring out the worst in us. By entering into a social contract, we give up our innate, natural freedom but should be exchanging it for a different kind of freedom. Unfortunately, all existing societies (he meant, in the mid-eighteenth century) enslave people without offering the freedoms we deserve. In a just society, laws are written and enforced for the greater benefit of all and by choosing to live in a society, accepting the social contract, we are freed. Indeed, we are 'forced to be free' in that we are forced to follow the laws that free us. Rousseau denied that we have individual rights; in the properly constituted state, they should not be needed as everyone benefits.

Rousseau claimed that society, by introducing us to the idea of wanting things other people have, leads us to be dissatisfied, envious, acquisitive and unhappy – states that don't exist in our 'natural' state.

The right to revolution

Occupying the middle ground between Hobbes and Rousseau, both David Hume and John Locke argued that a social contract, and by extension a society, must guarantee individuals the right to own and control property. When people come together to form a society, there is necessarily some sort of 'sovereign', or leadership. The

THE LEFT AND THE RIGHT

The opposing claims of the left- and the right-wing in politics reflect differing views of the role of society. The left-wing leans towards public ownership and public provision, with a top-down approach to fixing society so that it works. The extreme is Communism, with the 'means of production' owned by and operated for the benefit of the people. Right-wing policies favour private ownership, and a non-interventionist, laissez-faire attitude to social engineering in the belief that the free market will eventually lead everything to resolve

itself into an equilibrium that works. There is something of a Darwinian, evolutionary model of 'the survival of the fittest' to right-wing policies.

The assumption that eventually market forces will lead to equilibrium led to extreme hardship amongst the poor in Victorian London. What responsibilities does a society have towards its poorest members?

powers of the sovereign are limited by the rights to own and control property. If the government violates that first principle, the people have a right to rise up and revolt, overthrowing the government so that the principles can be re-established. The people might even have a duty to stage a revolution.

Who chooses?

Most countries aren't in a position to choose a form of government starting from a blank slate, but if they were, the American philosopher John Rawls (1921–2002) had just the solution. He proposed a theory known as Justice as Fairness to protect individual rights at the same time as promoting a fair allocation of resources. A new social order would be devised by people starting from what he called the 'original position' and working behind a 'veil of ignorance': they have to design the justice system without knowing what their own position in society will be. They could end up as the ruler, or as the lowliest worker or unemployed person.

Every post-apocalyptic movie, with or without zombies, has survivors ganging together, whether for good or evil intent: the first budding of a new society.

Chapter 20

Are some people more equal than others?

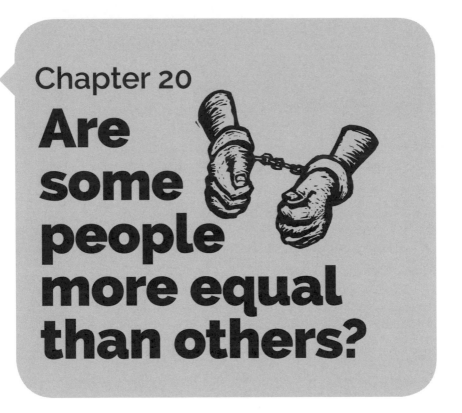

We claim to promote equality, but do we really?
And what is 'equality' anyway?

'Kindly remember that he whom you call your slave sprang from the same stock, is smiled upon by the same skies, and on equal terms with yourself breathes, lives, and dies.'
Seneca, first century AD

What do we mean by equality?

Equality in a society can mean many things. It can mean equal rights, equality of opportunity or equal access to resources, for instance. Most people today would say that everyone starts off with equal, basic human rights. Where do they come from? And what type of rights or equality do we really have?

The International Declaration of Human Rights sets out the kind of rights the modern world recognizes should be afforded to people:

• All human beings are born free and equal in dignity and rights. (Article 1)

• Everyone is entitled to all the rights and freedoms set forth in this Declaration, without distinction of any kind, such as race, colour, sex, language, religion, political or other opinion, national or social origin, property, birth or other status. (2)

• No one shall be subjected to torture or to cruel, inhuman or degrading treatment or punishment. (5)

• No one shall be subjected to arbitrary arrest, detention or exile. (9)

• Everyone, as a member of society, has the right to social

security and is entitled to... the economic, social and cultural rights indispensable for his dignity and the free development of his personality. (22)

And so on.

Are we born free and equal?

Aristotle noted that all people are *not* born equal. Some are born as slaves and born 'for' slavery, others born to be masters. But this, as

Slaves en route to the New World where they would be unable to enjoy life, liberty and the pursuit of happiness. They were 'possessions'.

Jean-Jacques Rousseau noted later, is to confuse cause and effect. A person born into slavery and raised as a slave will naturally become a slave, but if taken from slavery and slave parents at the moment of birth, he or she would be no different from another person. No one is genetically a slave.

Aristotle's thinking on slavery was soon challenged. The Stoics proposed the essential equality in rights of all people: 'We are born for Justice, and that right is based, not upon one's opinions, but upon Nature.' (Cicero)

The idea that social position is not an innate characteristic of an individual and cannot be fairly imposed on anyone, not even on those captured in war, was revolutionary.

> 'It is a mistake to imagine that slavery pervades a man's whole being; the better part of him is exempt from it: the body indeed is subjected and in the power of a master, but the mind is independent, and indeed is so free and wild, that it cannot be restrained even by this prison of the body, wherein it is confined.'
> Seneca the Younger, first century AD

Natural and inalienable rights

The idea that all people are born with natural and inalienable rights came to prominence during the Enlightenment. John Locke named them as the rights to 'life, liberty, and estate (property)' – the trio that were later enshrined in the US Declaration of Independence. Inalienable rights are those that cannot be surrendered or seized on entering into a social contract – the contract deemed to exist between citizen and government. The defences of slavery that relied on the claim that slaves had surrendered their rights voluntarily were considered invalid because these natural rights were not capable of surrender.

Other inalienable rights that have been suggested or claimed are the right to follow a faith and the right to one's own personality. There have been plenty of regimes that

> '[All people have] certain inherent natural rights, of which they cannot, by any compact, deprive or divest their posterity.'
> Virginia Declaration of Rights, 1776

have tried to strip away both proposed rights. Persecution of different faiths has been common throughout history, and attempts to suppress personality were a mark of totalitarian states in the twentieth century.

'Nonsense on stilts'

The idea that we have natural rights, or there are natural laws, relies on us accepting that there is something that is 'natural', something that is 'right' or 'justice' that exists 'out there'. In philosopherspeak, it relies on the existence of universals, or possibly on either a god or an entity called Nature which is laying down rights and rules.

> '*Every man is responsible for his own faith, and he must see it for himself that he believes rightly. As little as another can go to hell or heaven for me, so little can he believe or disbelieve for me; and as little as he can open or shut heaven or hell for me, so little can he drive me to faith or unbelief. Since, then, belief or unbelief is a matter of every one's conscience, and since this is no lessening of the secular power, the latter should be content and attend to its own affairs and permit men to believe one thing or another, as they are able and willing, and constrain no one by force.*'
> Martin Luther, 1523

Jeremy Bentham, who called the idea of natural rights 'nonsense on stilts', claimed that rights could only be created by government

or developed through tradition. This meant that there could be nothing inalienable about them as they have no special status. If they are not natural, they are also, then, culturally relative – they vary with time and place, and are different where there are different traditions and legal systems.

Is might 'right'?

For Bentham, rights only emerge when people are interacting, or entering into a social contract. If we imagine Robinson Crusoe secluded on his island, does he have rights? Does he have the right to take fish from the sea and fruit from the trees? Or are natural rights meaningless in his solitary state? When Friday turns up, does he have a 'right' to treat him as a servant? Or do rights not come into it?

Friday is on land that Crusoe is occupying – does that mean Crusoe owns it? Does the Declaration of Human Rights touch him, on his fictional island, giving him the right to own property? Does it give Friday the right to own any of the island?

Callicles, who lived in Athens 2,500 years ago, believed that the strong will and should predominate and that this is the only 'natural' state. Social Darwinism takes the idea of the 'survival of the fittest' and applies it to society (not in a way Darwin intended) to justify the triumph of the strong over the weak. If people have 'certain unalienable rights', where do they come from? If they are bestowed by society, they are neither universal nor natural.

Natural inequality

A quick look at the mass of humanity shows that even if we are born with equal natural rights we are not born with equal abilities. Some people are stronger than others, some better-looking than others, some cleverer or more musical than others. Our individual qualities and abilities are not equal and society values some above others.

> *'To measure "right" by the false philosophy of the Hebrew prophets and "weepful" Messiahs is madness. Right is not the offspring of doctrine, but of power. All laws, commandments, or doctrines as to not doing to another what you do not wish done to you, have no inherent authority whatever, but receive it only from the club, the gallows, and the sword. A man truly free is under no obligation to obey any injunction, human or divine. Obedience is the sign of the degenerate. Disobedience is the stamp of the hero.'*
>
> Leo Tolstoy's summary of the position presented by the Social Darwinist pamphlet *Might is Right,* 1890

Which qualities are valued varies between cultures. In the past, physical strength was a more valuable attribute than it is now that we don't have to fight off wild beasts or bring down prey animals for food. Some qualities which are valued might seem illogical: we pay professional sports players a lot of money; we value some actors, writers, painters and musicians highly. Playing the violin or making sculptures are hardly useful survival skills, but we value people who provide amusement, entertainment and art as well as those with practically useful skills. The very fact that we are *not* all equal in natural abilities creates value, and value produces further types of inequality.

CITY OF DURBAN
UNDER SECTION 37 OF THE DURBAN BEACH BY-LAWS. THIS BATHING AREA IS RESERVED FOR THE SOLE USE OF MEMBERS OF THE WHITE RACE GROUP.
STAD DURBAN
HIERDIE BAAIGEBIED IS, INGEVOLGE ARTIKEL 37 VAN DIE DURBANSE STRANDVERORDENINGE, UITGEHOU VIR DIE UITSLUITLIKE GEBRUIK VAN LEDE VAN DIE BLANKE RASSEGROEP.
IDOLOBHA LASETHEKWINI
NGAPHANSI KWESIGABA 37 SOMTHETHO WAMABHISHI ASETHEKWENI LENDAWO IGGINELWE UKUSETSHENZISWA NGAMALUNGU OHLANGA OLUMHLOPHE KUPHELA.

Equal opportunities?

A right to equal opportunities or equal treatment is not universally recognized but is enshrined in some legal systems. It provides that all people should be allowed to apply for a job, take a bus, dress

Do people have a natural right not to experience discrimination, or is it a socially constructed right? Or no right at all?

as they please, regardless of their colour, ethnicity, religious beliefs and so on.

Kant's view (see panel) seems fair, but it's very hard to achieve as all children start life from different positions and with different parents. Social authorities can't stalk into the houses of six-month-old babies to make sure they are being intellectually stimulated. We can't prevent some people having an advantage without violating other human rights.

From the 1920s to the 1970s, children in Israeli kibbutzim were raised communally, with only two or three hours a day with their parents. Nurit Leshem, who grew up on a kibbutz, says, 'We were educated to be the same; but we were, for all that, different.'

'Every member of the commonwealth must be permitted to attain any degree of status... to which his talent, his industry, and his luck might bring him; and his fellow subjects may not block his way [because of] hereditary prerogatives.'
Immanuel Kant

How far do you take the argument? Is it right for the rich to pay for better schooling for their children, giving them a clear, paid-for advantage that is not available to others? Some people believe it is, and others that it is not.

What's opportunity and how equal can it be?

It's difficult to define equality of opportunity. Does it mean access to the same things? Or access to the things that are most important or suitable to each individual? And who decides what that is? Equal opportunity to realize our personal potential will require unequal provision – the musical child will benefit from music lessons which might bring no benefit at all to a child who instead excels at sport.

As with any problem relating to existing societies, we are not starting from a level playing field. Some people have natural advantages by virtue of birth and some might have disadvantages for historical reasons. One answer to this is positive discrimination, or what Rawls calls 'fair equality of opportunity' to try to compensate for disadvantage. It's a controversial measure that raises objections – not least that it does exactly what it is meant to oppose – favouring one person over another on grounds of birth, ethnicity, gender, etc.

Political philosopher Robert Nozick (1938–2002) and economist Milton Friedman (1912–2006) both opposed equal-opportunity measures as they saw it restricting the right of others to employ

In a society otherwise intent on treating all citizens alike, the USSR had programmes to identify and nurture talent in sport and music – but for the glory of the state rather than self-realization of the individual.

whoever they choose and use their own property as they see fit.

Some are more equal than others

In his novel *Animal Farm*, George Orwell satirized the USSR under Stalin and Lenin, showing how a revolution which sought to make everyone equal quickly led to another oppressive society in which some people starved while others prospered.

Economists have found it impossible to create or even model a society in which horizontal inequality – inequality between people of equivalent abilities at equal starting points – does not emerge. Robert Nozick gave an example of how inequality emerges. (He used this to argue against trying to impose equality of wealth.) Suppose society begins with everyone owning $100 (£60). A sportsman –

the basketball player Wilt Chamberlain in his example – says he will only play in public if everyone who wants to watch pays 25 cents. By the end of the season, the

sportsman has $250,000 (£150,000) because many people wanted to watch him play. They have freely given their 25 cents. Why should we take any of it away from him? Equality of opportunity involves equal opportunities to succeed or fail, to become rich or poor, making it inherently incompatible with equality of outcome. Which would we prefer? Right-wing politics leans towards equality of opportunity and the left-wing towards equality of outcome.

Who are the people who are equal?

Many people in the economically developed world support equality of opportunity, yet want to limit the influx of immigrants. We legislate for the fair treatment of employees in our own lands, yet buy cheap goods made by workers in appalling conditions overseas. We say men and women have equal rights, people of different ethnic backgrounds have equal rights, and yet women on average earn less than men, black people earn less than white people and are more likely to go to jail. Do we really mean all people are born equal, or only 'people like us'?

Chapter 21

Should we rob one Peter to pay several Pauls?

How do we balance the benefits to the individual against those to the many?

In 2013, the Cypriot economy was in a dire state (as were quite a few other economies, if you recall). In an unprecedented and unpopular move, the Cypriot government decided to seize up to 60 per cent of bank deposits over 100,000 euros (£82,000, $138,000). The move particularly targeted Russian oligarchs who were using Cyprus as a tax haven, but inevitably it affected some ordinary citizens of Cyprus. Taking money from the richest depositers could potentially save a larger number of poorer Cypriots from greater hardship if the currency and banking sector collapsed. Does that make it right?

The greatest good for the greatest number

The principle of Utilitarianism can be used to defend the Cypriot cash-snatch.

Utilitarianism is based on the premise that actions are morally good or bad

> *'Actions are right in proportion as they tend to promote happiness, wrong as they tend to produce the reverse of happiness.'*
> John Stuart Mill, 1863

according to how far they maximize happiness and minimize pain. The actions that bring the greatest benefit to the largest number of people are chosen over alternatives.

'Happiness' is taken to mean pleasure and freedom from pain. Pleasure is not just wine, (wo)men and song, but includes higher intellectual pleasures. Utilitarianism is not an excuse for pursuing a life of self-indulgent hedonism.

Utilitarianism is unselfish and egalitarian – perhaps to a fault. Everyone's happiness counts equally, so sometimes, utilitarianism will require personal sacrifice.

> *'Pleasure, and freedom from pain, are the only things desirable as ends... all desirable things are desirable either for the pleasure inherent in themselves, or as means to the promotion of pleasure and the prevention of pain.'*
> John Stuart Mill

Most moral and legal codes, and even just good manners, are built at least approximately on a Utilitarian basis. It's generally best if we ban stealing, then we can all be fairly confident that we can reap the fruits of our labour and get along nicely. Otherwise, we'll spend a lot of time looking over our shoulders to see who's creeping up with the intention of pinching our mammoth kebab or tablet computer. (The same rules keep cropping up again and again.) On the whole, Utilitarianism seems to work reasonably well.

THE 'FELICIFIC CALCULUS'

It's not always immediately obvious which course of action will produce the greatest good. Jeremy Bentham (1748–1832), the originator of classic Utilitarianism, produced a 'felicific calculus' to help work out tricky problems of Utilitarian morality. This takes account of each pleasure and pain produced by an action and rates it for six qualities:

• Intensity
• Duration
• Certainty or uncertainty: how likely or unlikely is it to occur?
• Propinquity or remoteness: how soon will it occur?
• Fecundity: how likely is it to produce more sensations of the same kind?
• Purity: how likely is it to produce more sensations of the opposite kind?

The total points for pleasure and pain must then be multiplied by the number of people who will be affected in each way. If the final calculation shows a balance of pleasure, the act is approved. If it shows a balance of pain, the act is not a good idea.

People as trading tokens

There are several logical objections to Utilitarianism. One is that it seems inhumane, trading in human happiness as though it were a commodity in an economy. It would seem to condone the abuse

Jeremy Bentham was, at his own request, made into an auto-icon after death. His body was dissected, then the skeleton padded with straw and dressed. The head of the icon is a wax copy, as his real head looks rather ghoulish (between his feet) and is not usually displayed. Bentham occasionally sits in on meetings at University College London where he is marked as 'present but not voting'.

of the few by the many. If 100,000 Romans enjoy watching a slave torn apart by lions in the Coliseum, is the enjoyment of the audience enough to outweigh the agony of the slave? We could say that the slave's suffering is so immense it outweighs the pleasure of the happy spectators. Or we could say that the spectators are not enjoying true happiness, and the degradation involved in watching such an event would be more properly termed a pain than a pleasure.

But there are other cases – more useful in our own day and age – in which the common-sense answer to a question and the Utilitarian answer are at odds.

There are circumstances in which personal feelings might prevent someone doing the 'right' thing. Imagine you are held hostage with ten other people. The hostage-takers want to kill one particular person but can't identify that person. You know who it is. If no one identifies the target, they will kill half the hostages. If you identify the person, they will kill only that one individual. Will you identify the person? What if you were the person? What if your child or partner

> **THOUGHT EXPERIMENT: THE INHOSPITABLE HOSPITAL**
>
> Suppose five patients in a hospital all need vital organ transplants to live. A patient who is not critically ill comes in for a routine operation. The surgeon could kill the patient, make it look like a freak misfortune, and use his organs to save five other people. Is it immoral to kill one person to save five? Or should he heal the healthy patient and let the others die? Common sense tells us the surgeon should not kill the healthy patient. If asked why, most people would say something along the lines of it being random misfortune (bad luck) if the five die, but culpable murder to kill the healthy one, or that the surgeon doesn't have the right to decide who should live or die. But why not? Isn't he deciding anyway as soon as the possibility is clear to him? Isn't it equally bad luck to fall into the hands of an obsessively utilitarian surgeon?

was the person?

Utilitarianism would demand that you reveal the one person to save five, whoever it was. But your conscience, emotional involvement and self-interest are all likely to affect your decision. One problem with Utilitarianism is that it requires us to act according to clinical, mathematical logic – and people just aren't like that.

Negotiating with hijackers requires balancing currently endangered lives against the possible future consequence of more hijackings.

Peters and Pauls

All economic systems try to find a balance between taking money away from rich people and giving it to poorer people. Aiming for the greatest good to the greatest number is a good way of staying in power. In a democracy, people will not vote for a government that gets the balance wrong. In the worst case, the people will rise up to overthrow a government that gets it very wrong. If most people are happy, the government is likely to be stable. When most people are unhappy, things get difficult.

Protests in 2012 against austerity measures stressed that they represented the majority – 99%. Utilitarian principles would suggest that austerity measures should be abandoned, but governments introducing them claim they will stop greater misery in the future.

The general perception of the banking crisis that started in 2007 is that it was greed on the part of a small number of people that has caused misery to a large number of poorer people. The 99% movement claims to represent 99% of society – the portion who had not profited from the banking boom years. The use of the figure taps into people's natural utilitarian tendency to believe that the greatest benefit to the greatest number is the best way to calculate the morality of an act.

In 2007, just before the financial crash, the top 1% of the US population owned 43% of the wealth. The bottom 80% owned only 7% of the wealth.

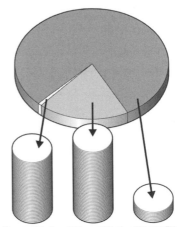

1% own 43% of total US wealth

19% own 50% of total US wealth

80% own 7% of total US wealth

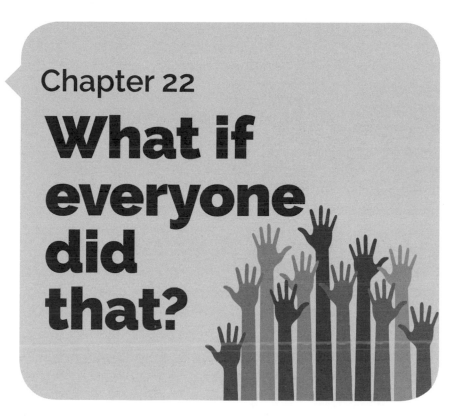

Chapter 22

What if everyone did that?

Society allows room for some renegades – but what would happen if we all wanted to be the odd one out?

The principle of the Golden Rule is that we should treat everyone the way we would like to be treated (see *Should we ever burn witches?* Page 172). Immanuel Kant had a similar principle, which he called the 'categorical imperative'.

Living virtuously

There have always been people who have tried to live the purest, most virtuous life. There are broadly two approaches – one is to spend one's life in the service of others or interacting honestly with them, and the other is to eschew the trappings of normal life and seek a form of enlightenment or tranquillity through contemplation or prayer. No philosopher seems to have taken an approach that involves owning four houses and a yacht.

'It is easier for a camel to go through the eye of a needle, than for a rich man to enter into the kingdom of God.'
King James Bible, Matthew, 19:23

The selfishness of selflessness

The Greek philosopher Diogenes (400–325BC) took the eschewing of the trappings of life to extremes. He was the ultimate ascetic. He set up home in a large pot in the marketplace and owned as little as he could get away with. He had a rag or two, and a drinking bowl. Or at least he had a drinking bowl to start with, but then when he saw a young boy drink from cupped hands he realized the drinking bowl was a luxury he could do without and dashed it to the ground. He didn't earn any money, as that would clearly be buying into the materialism he despised, and he lived on food he was given or that he found. Diogenes taught that the way to happiness was by living 'according to nature' – satisfying the body's most basic needs as simply as possible and shunning all possessions, personal ties and attachments. He demanded that his followers deliberately lay themselves open to scorn and ridicule as a practice in detachment.

As with monks and other religious ascetics, Diogenes depended on the generosity of others for his survival. Unlike monks, though, his dependent asceticism was not part of a wider, well-recognized spiritual scheme that might benefit the

whole community. It was a system he had devised himself for his personal enlightenment. This is all very well for Diogenes, but is it fair? He gets to be detached and enlightened, but only because other people are ready to give him food when he needs it (and leave suitable jars lying around in the marketplace).

How would it be if everyone stopped working, gave away their goods and looked for a jar to live in? Society would grind to a halt and there would be no more food or jars.

> *'Act only according to that maxim whereby you can, at the same time, will that it should become a universal law.'*
> Immanuel Kant, 1785

POLE DANCING, SYRIAN STYLE

The Stylites were early Christian ascetics who lived on top of columns or poles in the desert. The trendsetter was probably Simeon Stylites, who climbed his pillar in Syria in 423 and stayed there until his death 37 years later. There were variants. Theodoret of Cyrus, a contemporary of Simeon of Stylites, wrote of a hermit he had seen who had lived for ten years in a tub suspended from poles, and St Alypius is reported to have built a pillar and lived on it for 67 years. For the first 53 years he was standing up, but when his feet could no longer take the strain he lay down. It doesn't seem to have done him much harm as he is said to have lived to the age of 118.

Kant do that

Immanuel Kant would not have let Diogenes get away with it. His categorical imperative stated that any law by which we live our lives must be capable of being extended to everyone. So, as society would quickly collapse if everyone chose to live in abandoned jars, be provocative at best (antagonistic at worst) and do no productive labour, that is not a valid way to live.

But, of course, the problem doesn't arise. We don't see people scouring marketplaces looking for a jar to live in. We don't see them giving all their property to charity and cutting all their social ties. Most people don't want to live like Diogenes.

Does this mean that there is no place for begging ascetics? Perhaps that depends on the context. Medieval Europe saw many orders of wandering friars and monks who lived on charity and in return prayed for the souls of the society which provided for them. They traded prayer, which people considered a valuable commodity, for food and other necessities. Each person who gave to a begging friar did so of his or her own volition, and no doubt felt that their act of charity was ennobling or buying them some remission.

In some sense, the ascetic depending on charity is doing society a service – providing a useful conduit for charity which will be of spiritual benefit to donors. Even a philosopher spouting wisdom to anyone willing to listen, in exchange for food and a jar or pillar, is trading with the society he claims to despise. It works for only as long as there are enough people who want the spiritual or intellectual benefit provided by the ascetics in their midst, and not too many people who want to live in jars.

All for one, but not one for all

Kant's imperative is more usually applied to lifestyles that seem selfish in different ways. Life wouldn't work if everyone lived like a billionaire. In fact, we have recent evidence of that in the financial crisis that followed the banking disasters of 2008. Too many people were living 'like that' – in a way that their income or their society's productivity

could not support.

There are many systems that are based on the majority of people doing the 'right' thing. They range from social security benefit systems, which work as long as the majority pay in and those who take out are those in genuine need, to national vaccination programmes that control dangerous diseases by creating 'herd immunity'.

Society has room for some people to opt out of the communal good – it's not so fragile that it will collapse as long as the numbers are small. But does that give anyone the right to be the odd one out? Simeon Stylites and Diogenes did not live on state handouts – people gave freely, so it was a self-limiting system.

It seems that Kant is partly right – but perhaps he is asking too much. Life wouldn't work if we all wanted to be firemen, either.

Society works because people want different things. It can support a certain number of people who make very dependent choices – or have dependent needs – but in every society there is a critical balance. If we tip over the edge – all borrowing more than we can afford to pay back, for instance – disaster ensues.

MMR: A PRACTICAL LESSON IN THE CATEGORICAL IMPERATIVE

In 1998, a fraudulent paper published in the medical journal *The Lancet* claimed that the triple MMR vaccine to protect children against measles, mumps and rubella could lead to autism. As a result, the number of parents having their children vaccinated dropped. By 2008, measles was endemic in the UK (circulating in the general population) for the first time in fourteen years – a direct result of the drop-off in vaccination. The diseases that MMR protects against can cause lasting damage or death in children.

When enough people are vaccinated, the few who are not are protected by 'herd immunity' – the immunity of the majority which makes it very difficult for a disease to circulate. When insufficient people are vaccinated, all unvaccinated people become vulnerable. Did parents have the moral right to depend on herd immunity (at the cost of others) rather than accept the tiny risk they thought the vaccine presented? In fact, the vaccine does not produce autism – there was no risk – but the loss of herd immunity led to many cases of sickness and four deaths in the UK.

Chapter 23

Can a robot think for itself?
And should we be worried?

What are the limits of artificial intelligence?

There are plenty of science fiction films and stories in which artificially intelligent robots take over the world and then proceed to destroy human beings. Could it happen? Should we allow a state of affairs in which it could happen?

Primal fear?

The very first use of the word 'robot' came in the play *R.U.R.* by the Czech writer Karel Čapek – and in it a race of self-replicating robots, originally made as slaves, rebel and try to destroy humanity.

So the fear of the robots taking over is as old as the robots themselves. Unlikely as it may seem, is it really a genuine possibility?

THE THREE LAWS OF ROBOTICS

Science fiction writer Isaac Asimov set out the three laws of robotics in the short story 'Runaround', published in 1942:

1. A robot may not injure a human being or, through inaction, allow a human being to come to harm.
2. A robot must obey the orders given to it by human beings, except where such orders would conflict with the First Law.
3. A robot must protect its own existence as long as such protection does not conflict with the First or Second Law.

Later, Asimov added a zeroth law:

0. A robot may not harm humanity, or, by inaction, allow humanity to come to harm.

What would it take?

The usual scenario has people building robots that, whether deliberately on our part or not, become conscious. Then they rebel and cause havoc. They might be purely logical, and work out – say – that human beings are a bit of a nuisance, using up resources and doing dumb things like causing climate change.

> 'There is no security against the ultimate development of mechanical consciousness, in the fact of machines possessing little consciousness now. A mollusc has not much consciousness. Reflect upon the extraordinary advance which machines have made during the last few hundred years, and note how slowly the animal and vegetable kingdoms are advancing. The more highly organized machines are creatures not so much of yesterday, as of the last five minutes, so to speak, in comparison with past time.'
> Samuel Butler, *Erewhon*, 1872

Or they might become disgruntled at their low status, sick of doing mindless chores and being treated like slaves, and rebel in the way that real slaves might. The first option is available to any kind of independently intelligent robot; the second needs the robots to feel exploited or put-upon and aspire to something better – it needs a form of consciousness. Both require artificial intelligence – some reasoning or learning that goes beyond simple programming.

> **BANNED AI**
>
> As well as sci-fi scenarios in which the robots have taken over, there are those in which AI has been banned or defeated. In Frank Herbert's *Dune* series, a revolt 10,000 years before the start of the books, the Butlerian Jihad, saw humanity wipe out intelligent machines and ban their reinvention with the commandment 'Thou shalt not make a machine in the likeness of a human mind.'

The singularity

In 1993, mathematician Vernor Vinge proposed an event called the 'singularity' – the point where AI exceeds human capabilities and so can design ever better and more powerful versions of itself, quickly leading to intelligence far beyond our understanding. Then 'the human era will be ended'. The singularity is the starting point for sci-fi writers postulating machines taking over, destroying us, using us as slaves or even producing a paradise for us to live in. As they will be more intelligent than anything we can conceive of, we can't anticipate what they will do. The best prediction, which might be better called the best wild-stab-in-the-dark, for when this might come about is 2025–45, based on trends in developing computer capabilities.

What is intelligence?

There is no universally accepted definition of intelligence and so it's hard to say exactly what we mean by artificial intelligence (AI). Most people would say that it's not simply the ability to work things out by following rules – computers are already much better at that than we are. Intelligence seems to involve an ability to learn, to form creative leaps and to forge links or see connections that are not obvious. Human intelligence produces jokes and metaphors, picks up and uses nuance, interprets context and picks up clues from the behaviour of others.

Can a robot think for itself? And should we be worried? | **251**

In theory, an AI doctor-robot could make better and quicker diagnoses than a human doctor. It could store the details of millions of conditions and correlate symptoms to conditions and recommend a treatment.

But a human doctor can tell if the patient who is complaining of stomach ache is actually there because they are depressed, or if they are holding back information about a symptom because they are embarrassed or afraid. A computer won't pick that up.

THE TURING TEST

Computer pioneer Alan Turing (1912–54) proposed a test to determine whether AI had been achieved and whether a computer could be said to think like a human being. A computer passes the Turing test if a human interrogator can't tell it apart from a human in conversation. Turing believed it might be better to emulate the mind of a child and then educate the child-computer than to try to build a computer like an adult brain.

One objection to Turing's criterion is that it demands that machine intelligence is very similar to human intelligence. As Stuart Russell and Peter Norvig have pointed out, we don't demand that an aeroplane flies well enough to fool birds before we accept that it flies. Indeed, it was only when we gave up trying to copy birds that we made working planes.

How close are we?

Depending on who you ask, we either have genuinely intelligent and conscious computers already, or we are years away from achieving it.

Neurologists point to the complexity of animal brains and say that computers are nowhere near emulating anything but the simplest organisms. The whole of the internet is not as complex as the connections within a single human brain – and that's to say nothing of the things it can and can't do. On

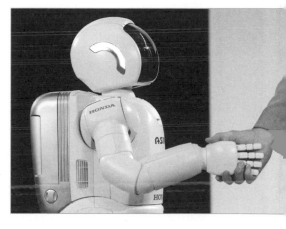

> 'If a machine behaves as intelligently as a human being, then it is as intelligent as a human being.'
> Alan Turing

the other hand, computer scientists point to ways they are modelling neurons and beginning to build 'brains' in a modular way, emulating the structure of real (but not necessarily human) brains and nervous systems. Some AI developers suggest that it is not necessary to try to mimic the brain to produce intelligence.

But would it be a brain?

Philosophers disagree about whether, if we could make an electronic replica of the human brain or an intelligent non-replica, it would 'count' as a brain or intelligent even if it could apparently perform the same functions.

John Searle suggested a thought experiment he called the 'Chinese room' to explain how AI does not have understanding.

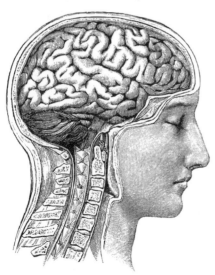

Imagine a person in a closed room who is passed questions written in Chinese. The person doesn't understand Chinese, but has a big book in which he can look up the questions and find suitable answers. He passes the answers back and to everyone outside the room it looks as if he can understand Chinese. AI, too, will be able to perform as though it had understanding but without actually having it. Searle distinguished between what he called weak AI and strong AI:

- 'A physical symbol system [effectively, a computer] can act intelligently' – this is weak AI.
- 'A physical symbol system can have a mind and mental states' – this is strong AI, and is the version that concerns philosophers.

The early AI developers assumed that the mind processes information in chunks according to certain rules and so this mechanism can be replicated by a machine. But unconscious instincts are key to human intelligence and expertise and these can't be reproduced in a set of rules or algorithms a computer could follow – hence the limitations of the AI doctor. Hubert Dreyfus, addressing this limitation of AI, said that true human intelligence and expertise is not 'knowing-that' (factual knowledge) but is 'knowing-how' (knowledge in action, as it were).

Turing pre-empted this objection and answered it by saying that

PHILOSOPHICAL ZOMBIES

The question of whether a machine can have a mind is a version of the 'problem of other minds'. This addresses the issues of whether we can be certain anything or anyone else has a mind. It's possible that you are the only minded being and everyone else is a flesh automaton, or philosophical zombie.

human intuitions might well follow rules, just rules that we haven't observed yet. In that case, they could at some point be emulated by machine intelligence. Since Dreyfus' work in the 1970s, research in AI has moved towards neural networks and evolutionary algorithms designed to deal specifically with the kind of unconscious processing, contexts and links that were not emulated in early models.

From thingness to being

It's one thing to be intelligent, but possibly a completely different thing to be conscious. Again, there's no consensus about what consciousness is or where/how it is located. John Searle suggests it emerges from a collection of neurons, just as the property of wetness emerges from a collection of water molecules (see page 79). In that case, an intelligent machine would also be a conscious machine.

Can we conceive of types of consciousness that are not like human consciousness? American philosopher Daniel Dennett claims that machines are already conscious, and that even a thermostat is 'conscious'. It's not a view many share. But if a machine has consciousness this opens a whole new Pandora's box of dilemmas. Could a conscious machine feel hope, despair, pain, anger, love, curiosity, envy, longing, pride? If so, does it have rights? And what responsibilities do we have towards such a thing? – or should that be 'such a being'? These questions have been explored most fully

ROBOTS IN LOVE

In the film *AI* (2001), directed by Steven Spielberg, a young boy AI called David has his 'imprinting protocol' initiated and loves the woman to whom he is a substitute son. This love can never be undone, and he still loves her 2,000 years later. What duties would we have towards robots that could love us?

In Japan, the government is offering 50–60 per cent subsidies for research and development to companies developing care robots for elderly people. Japan suffers from a serious shortage of care workers and robots might fill the gap. How should we feel about people becoming dependent on and perhaps emotionally attached to robots?

through science fiction writing and films rather than by routine sit-in-a-university-and-write-books philosophers.

How much power to give the machines?

The invasion of the killer robots is some way off, but there are many other ways in which we have made ourselves vulnerable by relying heavily on technology. The banking crisis that began in 2007/08 was largely caused by runaway computer algorithms. The Black–Scholes equation at the heart of trading had been used inappropriately to allow trading in derivatives (not a real product, just hypothetical money and prospects of profit) to reach a value of a quadrillion dollars a year. That's ten times the value of all actual stuff produced in the whole world over a century. As computers make decisions in a fraction of a second, things can get out of hand very, very quickly. Hand-in-hand with computers giving us the capability to make and do more, we have the chance that they will destroy more – and they don't even need to develop a malevolent intelligence to do it.

CAN WE LIMIT KNOWLEDGE?

Knowledge can bring benefits and dangers. Ever since the mythical Fall of Man, knowledge has been linked with danger. Knowledge of sub-atomic physics made nuclear weapons possible alongside the medical benefits of technologies such as MRI and CAT scans. Knowledge of the genome helps us improve crops and cure disease but could also give a terrorist or warmonger the ability to release a killer virus. Are there some types of knowledge that are just too dangerous to pursue? Should we limit research in some areas because of the potential for disaster, just as we limit it for ethical reasons? Or will that just make us powerless if an evil genius gets there ahead of us?

Killer robots are here

The use of drones – unmanned, computerized vehicles and weapons – in warfare is highly contentious. The argument of the armed forces is that 'our' soldiers are saved the dangers of a perilous mission over or into enemy territory. The argument against is that we are allowing technology to make the 'decision' to kill humans. Whether it is really a decision is debatable – the drone follows instructions to seek, identify and deal with a target.

The case for drones is largely utilitarian – it achieves the ends of killing a particular target (usually an insurgent hidden deep within enemy territory) effectively and with less danger of collateral damage (i.e. killing other people). But there is what philosophers call a 'fact-value' confusion here. The fact that it *is* easy to kill targets using drones doesn't mean that we *should* do it.

The case against drones addresses the utilitarian points and also takes a moral stance. Opponents point out that there have been accidental killings, and that it's not valid to argue for something on the basis of it being better than an alternative – such as wide-scale bombing – that was never proposed.

The case questions whether it is ever acceptable to use a method of killing that is so dissociated from human engagement, turning killing into something that can be done with a 'PlayStation

Drones violate the first two laws of robotics: they harm human beings, and they follow instructions even when those instructions will cause harm to human beings.

mentality'. This can be damaging psychologically and spiritually to those using drones, too. A report released by the Pentagon in 2011 revealed that 30 per cent of drone operators suffered burn-out as a result of 'existential crisis'. If pilots don't suffer existential crisis, they can be adversely affected in the opposite way, with killing becoming 'normalized'. Use of drones is also cloaked in secrecy, with targets chosen by top-level politicians and military leaders; lack of transparency might be a political and philosophical problem. Some philosophers argue, though, that ethics doesn't apply in the arena of war (see *Is all fair in (love and) war?* Page 199).

Chapter 24

Are we being watched or watched over?

Governments claim that surveillance is purely there to keep us safe from those who wish to do us harm. But at what cost?

There's hardly anywhere you can go in a town or city that there's not a CCTV camera peering at you. Add to that surveillance by government bodies of our emails, phone calls, texts and web activity and it can feel as if little of our lives is private. Does mass surveillance do anything useful? Is it good or bad? How can we balance protection and privacy?

You're on film

CCTV cameras serve two distinct purposes: deterrence and detection. They record activity in an area, providing possible

evidence that can help police investigations if a crime is committed. They also aim to deter people from committing a crime where the cameras can record it – why do something you know you'll be in trouble for? Whether CCTV cameras actually do reduce crime is disputed. Some experts say that better street lighting is as effective – but that's just another form of increasing visibility so for our purposes it is in some regards similar to CCTV.

Now you see it, now you don't

Are there crimes you would commit if you thought you

GUILT, SHAME AND FEAR

Someone might decide not to do a banned or immoral act because of:

- Fear of punishment. If fear is the only deterrent, they are likely to do the act if the threat of punishment is removed.
- Shame. Shame requires a public; we only feel shame if we know other people are aware that we have done something they disapprove of.
- Guilt. Guilt is private; we feel guilt if we regret something we have done, whether or not it has had adverse consequences or anyone else knows we did it.

Guilt is the mark of an internalized moral system; fear can exist without any awareness of morality. Shame, in the middle, requires an awareness of a moral system but does not require the perpetrator of the act to share the moral values of the system.

could get away with them? Maybe not big crimes, but little ones, like using an 'access only' road as a shortcut?

If there were a policeman standing at the end of the access-only road, few people would turn into it, knowing they could get into trouble. There's not likely to be a policeman there every day, though. Next time there isn't, people will use the shortcut again. Now, suppose that instead of standing still, the policeman was obviously walking up and down the road. Next time it looks as though there is no policeman, no one can be sure. Maybe he's just further down the street. Maybe there will still be trouble if you drive down there. So you take another route. The conclusion is counter-intuitive: the *possible* presence of a policeman is at least as good a deterrent, and possibly a better deterrent, than the *definite* presence of a policeman – because in the latter case, if the policeman isn't visible, he has no deterrent effect. A hard-pressed local authority could use the walking policeman to act as a deterrent on several roads because he doesn't have to be visible on any one of them still to have an impact.

Look out – they're all around you

The principle of the policeman who might or might not be there lies behind an experimental design for prisons proposed in the late eighteenth century by the philosopher Jeremy Bentham. The 'panopticon' is a circular structure, with each prisoner housed in a

cell facing in towards a
central observation tower.
A guard sits in the tower,
in a room with windows
all around but with blinds
obscuring the room from
outside observers. The
guard can see into any of
the surrounding cells, but
no one in a cell can see into
the watchtower. The effect,
according to Bentham, will be
that the prisoners will never know
when they are being observed, so will
be self-policing, acting always as though they are being observed.
A warren-like network of passages would allow guards to enter and
leave the watchtower unobserved, so there doesn't actually need to
be a guard present all the time – the deterrent effect of the potential
guard will be as great as if there is really someone watching.

Bentham advertised the panopticon as 'a new mode of obtaining
power of mind over mind, in a quantity hitherto without example',
which sounds gleefully oppressive. But he didn't intend his design
to be used as a means of oppression. Indeed, he was in favour of

individualism and promoted freedom of expression, the abolition of slavery and the death penalty, equal rights for women, the right to divorce and the decriminalization of homosexuality – pretty radical aims for the late-1700s. He called the panopticon 'a mill

for grinding rogues honest' – he saw it as a force for reforming and re-educating criminals:

'Morals reformed—health preserved—industry invigorated—instruction diffused—public burthens lightened ... all by a simple idea in Architecture!'

VIRTUAL PANOPTICON

In George Orwell's novel *Nineteen Eighty-Four* (1949), the population is subject to constant surveillance through 'telescreens' installed in all homes and public places:
'There was of course no way of knowing whether you were being watched at any given moment... you had to live... in the assumption that every sound you made was overheard, and, except in darkness, every movement scrutinised.'

Even so, the French philosopher Michel Foucault saw the panopticon as an icon of disciplinary power and the pervasive and invasive impulse to observe, and that is how it is generally considered.

Can you 'grind rogues honest'?

The prisoners in the panopticon might behave themselves, but surely only because they think they are being watched and fear punishment if they misbehave. This is not really making them honest, it is only making them obedient. Bentham might have argued that by always doing the right thing, the prisoners become accustomed to good behaviour and it becomes their default setting, as it were. Good behaviour becomes ingrained and automatic, and so they are reformed. We could see it rather as the way that a parent persists in making a reluctant child clean his teeth, and by adulthood tooth-cleaning is a habit no one questions.

> '*He who is subjected to a field of visibility, and who knows it, assumes responsibility for the constraints of power; he makes them play spontaneously upon himself; he inscribes in himself the power relation in which he simultaneously plays both roles; he becomes the principle of his own subjection.*'
> Michel Foucault, 1975

If all you want is a society of law-abiding citizens, perhaps automatic obedience is good enough. But Immanuel Kant would disagree. Although in favour of people obeying the moral law because it is the law, he wanted them to obey it because they *wanted* to – because they wanted to be good, moral citizens.

Unthinking obedience is not the mark of a moral person. Indeed, constant surveillance and fear of consequences could be a bad thing. It stunts our growth as moral individuals; we become morally flabby as we are not exercising our judgment, reflecting on our behaviour, challenging our actions and the rules by which we live.

Unthinking obedience to authority can have dire consequences; for a healthy society, people must take responsibility for their moral choices and challenge decisions that are made in their name, for example the setting up of concentration camps.

Simply internalizing the rules, which Bentham considered a benefit in producing obedient citizens, Foucault saw as making individuals responsible for their own subjugation.

SHOULD YOU FILTER THE INTERNET FOR YOUR CHILDREN?

There has been a lot of concern lately about online content that is unsuitable for children. Some people use filtering software to prevent their children accessing violent or sexual content, either accidentally or on purpose. The danger of the child being upset or damaged by what they see must be set against the need for the child to develop self-regulating behaviour. For many people, that means that the online activity of younger children will be monitored and regulated, but the restrictions and protections should decrease as children grow and need to take responsibility for themselves. A parent who over-protects a child leaves that child ill equipped for independent life.

'If you're not guilty you have nothing to hide'

In 2013, the American computer specialist Edward Snowden revealed the wide-ranging surveillance of ordinary citizens through their online activity by authorities in the USA, the UK and Israel. Snowden uncovered intrusion on an unprecedented level, and more soon emerged – including allegations that the USA spied on major European political figures including the German Chancellor and the Pope. Wanted for espionage and theft of government property, Snowden fled the USA.

The case reopened a long-running debate about privacy and security. On the one side, authorities who want to observe the public claim that if you have nothing to hide, you shouldn't be worried about being observed. On the other side, people who object to being watched say that if they are not doing anything wrong they have a right to privacy. The public is divided into those who are comforted by security measures and those who are affronted by them.

> '*You can't have 100 per cent security, and also then have 100 per cent privacy and zero inconvenience.*'
> US President Barack Obama, 2013
> **Some commentators have challenged the view that it has to be a choice between privacy and security, and have asked for security measures which do not invade privacy.**

Justifying surveillance

The American philosopher Emrys Westacott has suggested that the morality of surveillance is determined by:

- whether there is a justified cause
- the means used
- whether the surveillance and degree of intrusion is in proportion to the risk that surveillance is supposed to guard against.

In addition to these factors, the watched citizen worries about the

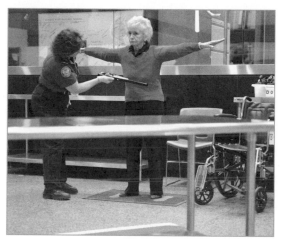

Some people object to increased security checks at airports; others welcome them, finding them reassuring.

security and accuracy of the information collected, and whether it might be misused. It looks as though all the cards are in the hands of the authorities, but that's not quite true. In a democracy, governments have to retain the trust of the people in order to stay in power. People who are not trusted and respected don't give their trust and respect in return.

In assessing whether they feel surveillance is justified, and so whether they are willing to tolerate the invasion of their privacy, people will think first about who is being protected. We are most tolerant of surveillance that we believe is for our own protection. This is the line that has been pushed by the authorities in the USA and UK: that the increased level of surveillance increases the security of the general population. Sometimes the surveillance is intended to protect the government. In the worst case, it is to protect individuals in a

Intruding the baby's privacy with a monitor is generally considered acceptable because it is entirely for the baby's protection – though it also provides peace of mind for the parent or carer. It's also deemed that the baby has no need of privacy, though the growing child is afforded more and more privacy.

government. At that point, the population is likely to be least sympathetic to the erosion of privacy as it is not a fair deal – the public gets little benefit from the loss of privacy.

Just a number

For some people, the role of technology in the surveillance of private communications makes the whole issue more sinister. When people are treated as data, they feel affronted, undervalued and stripped of human dignity. With plenty of experience of human/computer error in other areas, many of us fear the harm a miscalculation or wrong algorithm could do. Surveillance then becomes not only about the erosion of privacy but about the erosion of power and even our sense of personhood, and the value of that personhood.

Chapter 25

Should you rock the boat?

Is it best to assume the majority view is right? Or does the boat need rocking sometimes?

A lot of people will do almost anything for an easy life, and find it hard to cope with someone whose ideas are outside the mainstream. 'Don't rock the boat', we're told if we ask an awkward question. 'Go with the crowd.' 'Sixty million (or a hundred million, or a billion) people can't be wrong.' Well, why can't they?

A brief history of being wrong

Progress comes when people find a better way of doing things, or a better model or theory. Long ago, everyone thought the sun went round the Earth. We used the highly toxic metal mercury to treat syphilis. People kept slaves

> *'Have the courage to go against the tide.'*
> Pope Francis, 2013

and abused women. Pandas were thought to be mythical. And what about all the people who have believed in completely different sets of gods through the ages? They can't all have been right. The number of people who hold a belief is no guarantee that the belief is true.

Leaps and bounds

Thomas Kuhn (1922–96) suggested that science goes through long periods when no one challenges the prevailing models, and then brief periods of radical change or paradigm shift. Most of the time, no one deviates far from standard thinking. It is when someone thinks 'outside the box' that significant progress is made. Often the people who make these big leaps are disbelieved or ridiculed to start with, such is the power of popular opinion.

The astronomer Mikolaj Kopernik (Copernicus) published in 1543 his theory that the Earth goes around the sun. More than seventy years later, the

Catholic Church decided the idea was 'foolish and absurd... and formally heretical', and demanded that Galileo stop teaching it. The geocentric model was so widely accepted before Copernicus that it had the status of consensus reality – it was effectively real by virtue of being so widely believed.

Die rather than lie

The Greek philosopher Socrates made himself very unpopular by questioning the people of Athens about their beliefs and ideas. He would stop people in the marketplace and challenge them to define concepts such as virtue or justice. He quickly showed them that their unconsidered, received opinions didn't really work. He was soon in trouble for corrupting the youth of Athens, as well as being an irritant, and told that he had to stop teaching philosophy. Socrates refused, saying he would rather die a thousand times over than stop telling the truth and practising philosophy. He was convicted and told to drink poison to carry out his own execution (but only once).

An easy life

We're all brought up with certain beliefs. If it ever occurs to us that they could actually be wrong, we might or might not challenge them because we tend to believe that if lots of people think something, they are almost certainly right. Most people also prefer to be liked –

or at least not to be ridiculed.

Socrates recommended that instead of just taking on board all the ideas that are current and unquestioned in society, we should hold each up to scrutiny and decide, through investigation and logical thought, whether we really believe the idea to be true or just. He considered that to hold and defend an opinion you have not thought about is to opt out of the main benefit of being human.

Turning against the tide: whistle-blowing

As children, we all learn to hate a snitch – someone who gets the others into trouble by 'grassing' on them to teachers or parents. The

> 'The unexamined life is not worth living.'
> Socrates

misdemeanours involved are generally small, and often accidental. Who broke the window? Who let the class hamster out? Who wrote rude words on the board? It's considered to be fraternizing with the enemy (grown-ups) to uncover the culprit. This attitude persists. It's formalized in the criminal world, where a grass can expect a nasty

Going along with what other people tell you to think can lead to bad results.

fate if discovered. And how many of us have frowned on criminal behaviour but not reported it?

A whistle-blower exposes corruption, malpractice or dodgy dealing in an organization, in the public interest. Whistle-blowers are often reviled, persecuted and can suffer dire consequences for their public-spirited actions. Although many countries have laws to protect whistle-blowers, it's very often the case that those who do report wrong-doing in an organization – especially a government organization – pay a high price.

Self-interest v. communal-interest

The utilitarian principle requires us to weigh up the costs and benefits to everyone who will be affected by a decision and choose the option that brings the greatest total happiness. Generally, this should mean that we would blow the whistle if it would mean people being saved from danger or abuse. But self-interest usually affects our choices. If you were in a sinking ship and could choose between saving your own partner or two strangers, you would almost certainly save your own partner. To make such a disinterested choice that you saved the two strangers would not even win you any friends as it is so inhuman.

Accountancy of sacrifice

Some exploitative organizations and individuals depend on our self-interest to keep their bad practices hidden. A person who blows the whistle on an employer might lose their job, or be persecuted at work. They might lose their workplace friendships and status.

Many lose their homes, families, health and even lives in the subsequent stream of lawsuits and aggressive or vindictive responses. In many cases, the whistle-blowing does not even achieve the result

HERO OR TRAITOR?

American Edward Snowden released documents to the media revealing the extent of US surveillance of private citizens, including the use of data from Facebook and Google. He was accused of treason and fled the country.

'My sole motive is to inform the public as to that which is done in their name and that which is done against them.'

Is he a traitor, turning people against actions the government considers necessary security measures, or a hero for standing up for the privacy and disclosure rights of law-abiding individuals?

His life is in ruins and he may serve a long term in jail. Was he a martyr or a fool?

intended, as the whistle-blower is discredited and can't fight the massive resources of the organization.

Tribal loyalties

People feel loyalty to any group they belong to.

> **'You either become complicit, or you challenge it.'**
> Michael Woodford, ex-president and CEO of Olympus who uncovered and revealed payments to Yakuza, the Japanese mafia, by high-ranking Olympus bosses

Whistle-blowing entails a conflict of loyalties because our loyalty to the smaller, more immediate group (our co-workers and employers, for instance) is at odds with our loyalty to the larger community. When those who stand to benefit from the whistle-blowing are very remote – workers in a factory in Bangladesh, for instance – the cost

to our more local 'tribe' might seem to outweigh the benefit to people we don't know and will never meet.

> **'The question of conscience is a matter for the head of the state, the sovereign.'**
> Adolf Eichmann, at his trial in Jerusalem, 1962

Conscience triumphs

When a whistle-blower takes the decision to come clean about some abuse or crime, they are following their conscience rather than a set of rules, guidelines or loyalties that would encourage them to stay silent. According to evolutionary biologist Charles Darwin (1809–82), conscience evolved for precisely this reason – to help us resolve conflicts between self-interest and the interests of society in a way that will aid the preservation of the whole community. On an individual level, it leads us to avoid behaviours that bring shame and that are detrimental to society.

> **'The private conscience is not only the last protection of the civilized world, it is the one guarantee of the dignity of man.'**
> Martha Gellhorn, 1962

Conscience is not always considered a rational faculty, but more a 'gut instinct' – though that may come about as a result of long-term indoctrination in a particular moral scheme. This results in the feeling that it would be 'right' to reveal abuse even though reason says

Whistle-blowers often end as martyrs. Chelsea (previously Bradley) Manning was sentenced to 35 years in prison for making public documents and videos she had access to as a US soldier. These included footage of a US helicopter in 2007 firing on unarmed civilians in Iraq, including a journalist.

that it will probably have bad consequences for the whistle-blower. Other philosophers, including St Thomas Aquinas (1225–74), do see conscience as an application of practical reason. Some see it as given directly by God. But conscience is clearly fallible as we see when people employed by despotic regimes to oppress and torture others do not consider their acts to be wrong.

'Preserve a quiet conscience and you will always have joy. A quiet conscience can endure much, and remains joyful in all trouble, but an evil conscience is always fearful and uneasy.'

Thomas à Kempis, *The Imitation of Christ*, c.1418

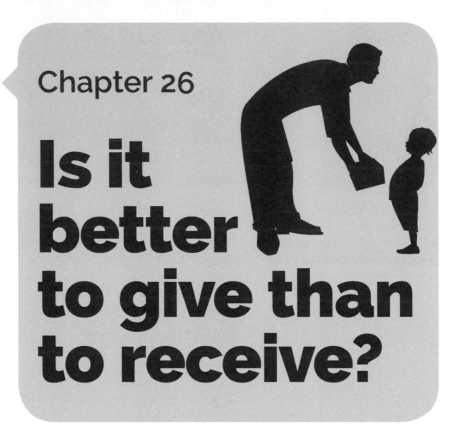

Chapter 26

Is it better to give than to receive?

For every gift there must be a donor and a recipient. Is one better than the other?

Is it better to give than to receive? And if so, how much is it better to give? Who benefits more from charity – the donor or the recipient?

Giving because you want to or because you have to

One of the five pillars of Islam is 'zakah'. This is a duty to pay 2.5 per cent of surplus wealth (money left after paying for essentials and taxes) as a contribution to help the poor. It serves two purposes – to make the Muslim reflect on the nature of wealth and avoid becoming too fond of material goods, and to redistribute wealth, helping the poor. It is considered neither a tax nor a charitable donation. The penalty for non-contribution is stiff:

'If any owner of gold or silver does not pay what is due on him, when the Day of Resurrection would come, plates of fire would be beaten out for him; these would then be heated in the fire of Hell and his sides, his forehead and his back would be cauterized with them. Whenever these cool down,

(the process is) repeated during a day the extent of which would be fifty thousand years.'

So this much the Muslim must do. But in addition, Muslims are encouraged – but not obliged – to make donations to 'sadaqah', or charity. People with no religious or social obligation to give to the needy might still give generously to charity. They might feel that they have a moral obligation to do so even though there is no formal duty. Is there any difference in giving without obligation?

Values and duties

Philosophers often identify two different aspects of virtue: values and duties.

Values are the more open-ended and apply to states or people; duties are specific and relate to acts. So we could say that Gandhi was a virtuous man, and that helping an injured person is a social duty. There is, of course, often overlap. A compassionate person will be more willing to discharge their duty to help someone who is injured. A duty may be an act one feels morally obliged to perform or one imposed by a rule.

A question then becomes how much we should do?

Can you ever do enough?

If you decide to buy a hat, or go on holiday, or spend your time watching television, you are doing so at the expense of choosing to give your money and time to a charity. The charitable acts and donations would certainly bring greater total benefit than a new hat, a holiday or watching TV for the evening, so are the 'right' choice. But we don't and won't all give up small personal gratifications to give all to charity. Two brands of consequentialism try to let us off the hook. Progressive consequentialism says we should act to make the world better than if we did nothing, but we don't have to do everything we can to improve it. Satisficing consequentialism says we should produce enough good – so we don't have to give all to charity as long as we give some, and we don't do harm with the time and money we are not giving.

Suppose a person has an income of $50,000 (£30,000). They want to help the poor. The obvious answer is to give their $50,000 away, but that won't really work. They will then be so poor that they need the help of others in the form of donated food, shelter and clothing. So perhaps they take out their necessary living costs and give away the surplus. Is that any good? Well, maybe. But now they don't have smart clothes and maybe won't be given a promotion that would come with a higher salary (allowing them to give away more). Perhaps by maintaining a certain level of spending and socializing, they can associate with other wealthy people and persuade them

FOR THE PRICE OF A PAIR OF SHOES...

Australian philosopher Peter Singer (born 1946) presents this question to highlight the way in which geographic distance affects our charitable impulse.

If you saw a child drowning in a pond, you would, presumably, jump into the pond and save the child, even if it meant ruining a good pair of shoes. Few people would think the life of a child not worth the cost of a pair of shoes.

So if you have opportunity, through a charity, to give the price of a pair of shoes to save the life of a child in a distant country, why might you hesitate to give? What makes the child in front of you more worthy of saving than the child 10,000 km away?

to give to charity, too. A person who gives only $5,000 (£3,000) but encourages ten friends to give $2,000 (£1,200) each has contributed more than a person who gives $16,000 (£10,000).

Should you shave your head or grow a moustache?

Years ago, giving to charity was a private and usually anonymous act. It still can be – you can drop money into a collecting box, give anonymously online or by text message or even endow a foundation that doesn't bear your name. But it's also now increasingly common to make a public display of generosity. The boring old sponsored walk has been replaced by sponsored grow-a-moustache, sponsored head-shaving, sponsored abseiling and sponsored holidays (marathons in foreign countries, helping turtles into the sea on distant beaches, and so on).

Of course, no one will sponsor (or applaud) you for something if they don't know you're doing it. While it was easy to sneak off and do a walk or swim, suddenly shaving your head or growing a moustache is a very public act. The public display increases the funds raised for charity, but it also increases the exposure of your own generosity. It's very 'look at me'. Does that make any difference to the validity of the gesture? Or is it all the same, as long as the money comes in and goes to the needy? How much do the intentions and the gesture matter?

Practising virtue until it comes naturally

Aristotle would have liked us to give to act well because we are spurred by virtue to do so, not so that other people will be impressed by our generosity or we can feel good about ourselves. Natural feelings of compassion and generosity should make us want to help others with no thought for the effect it has on ourselves (as long as the effect is not so detrimental it means we then need help from others). But what if you don't feel virtuous? Is it still good to give? It seems that it is. The people on the receiving end of your good behaviour will benefit and you will be building up your virtue-muscle by acting in the right way. Eventually, virtuous practice becomes ingrained and slowly automatic, if Jeremy Bentham was correct (see *Are we being watched or watched over?* Page 261). It's a bit like exercise. You might really dislike it to start with, but after a while it becomes enjoyable and a part of your life. That, according to Aristotle, is when you count as virtuous (not when you like running, but when acting virtuously is your default setting).

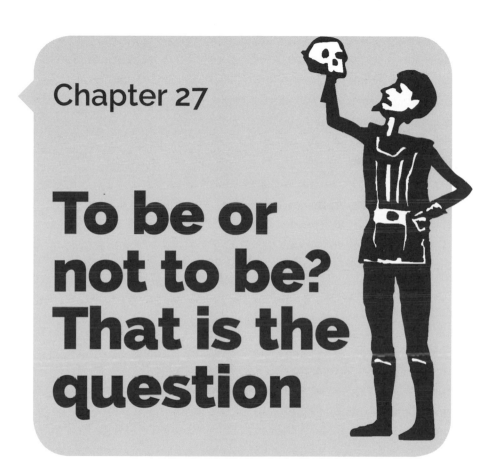

Chapter 27

To be or not to be? That is the question

Facing the slings and arrows of outrageous fortune...

'To be or not to be?' so asks Hamlet in his famous speech. The question is not just whether suicide is justified, or acceptable, but whether it is 'nobler' to suffer or to kill oneself. It's not really a question to tackle in a moment of overwhelming personal crisis, but is one for a more contemplative mood.

God-given life

For many people, religious beliefs deny them the right to choose suicide. If your god has forbidden self-murder, and you accept the teachings of that god, the question doesn't arise. Move along, please; nothing to see here.

> *'God's command "Thou shalt not kill," is to be taken as forbidding self-destruction.'*
> St Augustine, 345–430

Or is there?

Well, there is always the question of what actually constitutes suicide, and that might be quite important to a person of faith. A reasonable definition of suicidal behaviour would be that a person willingly and knowingly undertakes an action intended to kill them. We might allow it to be at one remove – so asking a doctor to administer a lethal dose of a drug could be suicide. On the other hand, running into a burning building in the hope of saving a child, but dying as a consequence, is not suicidal behaviour as the rescuer did not intend to die. Even though the person might know death is a *likely* consequence, as it is not the *intended* consequence, it can't be called a suicide. Accidentally taking an overdose of a prescription drug is not suicide, but taking it deliberately is. Deliberately taking an overdose but taking too little to die is suicidal behaviour but is not a successful suicide. Here there is a grey area, though. Sometimes, people make rather ambivalent suicide attempts that are instead suicidal gestures. Do they actually want to die? Some suicides are probably failed suicidal gestures – in that they fail to be a gesture and end in death. Intention, knowledge and outcome all have to come together (see *Does 'I didn't mean to' make a difference?* Page 187).

It's not only religious believers who cite the sanctity of human life as a reason for condemning suicide. But if we are to accept that human life is always special, no matter how much suffering it involves, the argument must logically be extended

Is life a gift that can't be refused? If the life you have been 'given' is intolerable, you don't have to be grateful. A gift is not truly given if the donor still claims some ownership or authority over it, so the 'gift' argument doesn't hold up – you are free to dispose of a gift you don't like or want.

to ban all killing. That includes judicial execution, the shooting of an armed criminal threatening others, the slaughter of warfare, and letting someone in pain slip into death if they want it rather than extending their life artificially. Few people are willing to sign up to a completely uncompromising position.

Putting up with it all

For the ancient Greek philosophers, suicide was generally considered to be disgraceful and the coward's way out. Plato suggested that it was tantamount to going AWOL – leaving the position the gods had assigned to you as a punishment for your misdeeds. But he did allow some exceptions, including madness, extreme torment, shame at having acted immorally, and the compulsion of judicial suicide.

For the Stoics, including Seneca (4BC–AD65), endurance was a virtue and led to a better life. They taught that we should try to

'Not only is suicide a sin, it is the sin. It is the ultimate and absolute evil, the refusal to take an interest in existence; the refusal to take the oath of loyalty to life. The man who kills a man, kills a man. The man who kills himself, kills all men. As far as he is concerned he wipes out the world.'
G. K. Chesterton, *Orthodoxy,* 1908

9/11: THE 'FALLING MAN' AND THE NOT-JUMPERS

During the terrorist attack on the Twin Towers on 11 September 2001, 200 people fell or jumped from the windows. The official record of the New York City medical examiner's office gives the cause of death as 'homlclde by blunt trauma' (i.e. impact with the ground) and not suicide. They are not listed as 'jumpers' because, 'Jumping indicates a choice, and these people did not have that choice. That is why the deaths were ruled homicide, because the actions of other people caused them to die.'

This account doesn't satisfy all relatives of the not-jumpers. For some, suicide is a sinful act which will bring divine retribution, no matter what the circumstances. For others, though, the thought that their loved one did have some control, did make one final choice, is comforting. For those relatives, it is 'nobler in the mind' to end one's troubles.

Attempts to identify the 'falling man' in this iconic photo from 9/11 were hampered by some families refusing to consider that their loved one might have chosen jumping over burning to death. They believed that suicide would lead to damnation.

accept the things that happen to us and respond with reason and moderation, achieved by learning fortitude and self-control. They did not deny extreme emotional states, but sought to transform them, and so attain calm. According to Epictetus, the Stoic can be 'sick and yet happy, in peril and yet happy, dying and yet happy, in exile and happy, in disgrace and happy'.

The Stoic way does not actually rule out suicide. It was considered permissible in cases of extreme pain or disease, or if it was impossible, because of circumstances, to live a virtuous life – if one were oppressed by a tyrant, for instance. In other words, if a

> *'When a man's circumstances contain a preponderance of things in accordance with nature, it is appropriate for him to remain alive; when he possesses or sees in prospect a majority of the contrary things, it is appropriate for him to depart from life.'*
> Cicero, 106–43BC

wise man would when exercising reason consider suicide the best option, it was permissible. As the Stoics considered some things essential to well-being, including health and freedom, lack of those could also be grounds for suicide. Seneca said that the wise man 'lives as long as he ought, not as long as he can'. That's not the same thing as plunging from a bridge in a fit of despair after the end of a love affair.

The problem of coercion

If a captured spy fears that she will be tortured and so takes a cyanide capsule, is that suicide? Assuming that the spy would not otherwise have sought to die, but does it to escape either the pain of torture or the possibility of betraying her country under torture, she has been coerced into killing herself.

Must coercion be by a person? Someone with a painful terminal condition who would not otherwise want to die could say they are coerced by circumstances. Most people who kill themselves do it to escape something – perhaps a terrible situation or mental anguish. If they could escape their torment without dying they would probably do so. Are they any more 'guilty' of suicide than the spy facing torture or the man jumping from the North Tower on 9/11?

Thinking the unthinkable

For centuries, the prevailing view in Christian Europe was that suicide is an unpardonable sin. Thomas Aquinas had three objections to suicide, one being the interesting notion that it is presumptuous – it takes the decision of when to end our life out of God's hands and so usurps his authority. (This is reminiscent of Plato thinking suicide resembled desertion.) It was only when religion began to lose its stranglehold over the issue that philosophers could once again

The Romantic movement glorified the idea of suicide as the inevitable response of the anguished soul disappointed in love or life.

contemplate the validity of suicide as an option.

The ancient Greeks had considered suicide more in terms of social duty and duty to the gods than in terms of a personal dilemma. David Hume addressed the social issue – one that still concerns people today – from a utilitarian standpoint. He proposed that if continuing with life is a painful burden for the individual, they are unlikely to be contributing a great deal to society, so the loss to society if that person dies is probably quite small and outweighed by the benefit to the individual in release from it. There are cases in which the utilitarian equation would argue against suicide – when it would leave grieving orphans to be cared for at public expense, perhaps. But some suicides will have little social impact – if the person leaves no surviving family, for example. In each case, the harm to the suicidal person of continuing to endure a life of anguish must be weighed against the harm to others (individuals or the community) to determine whether that particular suicide was morally wrong. Against the argument that suicide violates the social contract, the would-be suicide could say that society has already reneged on the deal if life is intolerable.

Enduring the unendurable

The existentialists, best known for smoking and drinking coffee in Parisian cafés in the twentieth century, identified the 'absurd' fact that human life is meaningless, there is no God, no purpose to what we do, and that ultimately all is vanity and death. It's called 'absurd' not because it's ridiculous but because it renders life and the search for meaning absurd. The anxiety, or angst, that comes from the recognition of our impotence and insignificance is a deep philosophical despair.

So – if it's all going to end in tears anyway, why not end it all now? The conclusion that life is therefore pointless and not worth the bother is one Albert Camus struggled to avoid. In the end, he said, we have to live in spite of that knowledge: 'The struggle itself is enough to fill a man's heart.' Using the analogy of Sisyphus, condemned forever in Greek myth to push a heavy boulder up a mountain and then have it roll back down, he concluded that the way forward is to 'imagine Sisyphus happy' – that is, accept the situation and find it liberating – live within the freedom it gives us.

Suicide as a duty

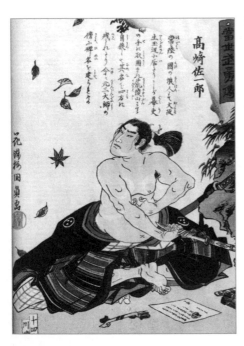

Philosopher John Hardwig makes a controversial claim that in some cases people have a moral obligation to kill themselves. If their continuing life is so burdensome to others that ending their life would produce greater

For a Japanese samurai defeated in battle, shamed or condemned to death, ritual suicide by disembowelling was a moral duty. Known as sepukku, or hara-kiri, it was performed by cutting across the abdomen using a special knife.

benefit in total than continuing, they should opt for suicide. He does not go as far as to say others should kill these troublesome survivors. However, he did concede: 'I can readily imagine that, through cowardice, rationalization, or failure of resolve, I will fail in this obligation to protect my loved ones.'

'No one wants to die. Even people who want to go to heaven don't want to die to get there. And yet, death is the destination we all share. No one has ever escaped it, and that is how it should be, because death is very likely the single best invention of life. It's life's change agent. It clears out the old to make way for the new.'

Steve Jobs (1955–2011)

There is no conclusion

Philosophy is an unending endeavour. Once you start to think about the myriad questions which life throws up, it's impossible to stop. Even if you reach answers that you are happy with to some of the questions, you will always find more questions to ask. But the one, truly important question that everyone should address is, 'what do I think?' Everything follows from that. To return again to Kierkegaard: *'The thing is to find a truth which is true for [you], to find the idea for which [you] can live and die.'*

Philosophy is a quest for truth. If we see it as a quest for absolute truth, we won't get to the end of the journey – but that's not the same as failing. If we see it as a quest for 'a truth which is true for [you]', you just might reach the end of your journey. You might even recognize it when you get there.

And we should give the last word to Sophocles, who set the ball rolling for Western philosophy. Remember, 'The unexamined life is not worth living.'

Picture Credits

Aleš Tošovský: 45. Clipart: 241, 281. Corbis: 78 (Rick Friedman), 107 (Bettmann), 113 (ClassicStock), 156, 185 (Bettmann), 200 (Oliver Coret/In Visu), 204 (Bettmann), 205 (Tarker), 235 (Hulton-Deutsch Collection). David Woodroffe: 238b. Dhatfield: 35. Friman: 266. Getty Images: 124. Guinnog: 226. Ken and Nyetta: 74. Kobal Collection: 5, 257. Pearson Scott Foresman: 192. Press Association Images: 295 (Richard Drew/AP). NASA: 31, 135. Shutterstock: 4, 6, 8, 9, 12, 13, 15, 17, 22, 29, 33, 36, 38, 41, 43, 44, 47, 48, 50, 53, 56, 57, 60, 61, 63, 65, 67, 68, 71, 73, 76, 80, 82, 84, 86, 89, 90, 96, 98, 100, 103, 106, 108, 112, 117, 118, 119, 127, 130, 133, 136, 137, 139, 140, 142, 144, 146, 147, 149, 152, 154, 157, 158, 159, 161, 164, 166, 168, 170, 172, 178, 181, 184, 187, 189, 190, 195, 197, 199, 201, 206, 207, 212 (africa924), 215, 217, 218, 222, 229, 231, 232 (yakinii), 237 (Wally Stemberger), 238t (Peeradach Rattanakoses), 239, 245, 247, 249, 251, 253 (catwalker), 254, 260, 261, 262, 271 (Carolina K. Smith), 272, 273, 277, 280 (Bocman1973), 283 (Kobby Dagan), 284, 285, 286, 289 (Mr Pics), 291, 293, 301, 303. Wellcome Images: 69, 216, 220, 298.